T5-AQR-406

Bible Nurture and Reader Series

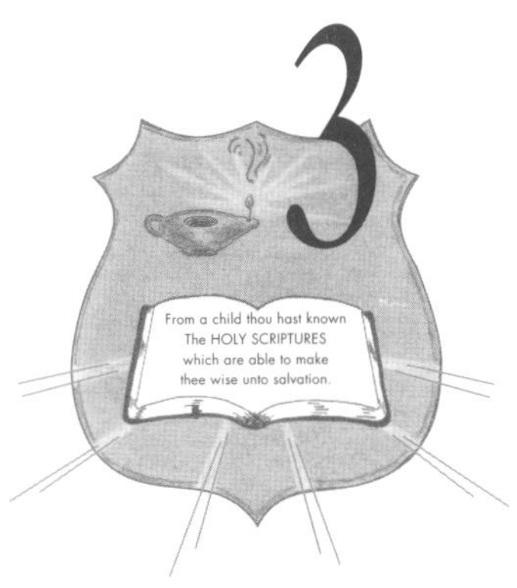
3
From a child thou hast known
The HOLY SCRIPTURES
which are able to make
thee wise unto salvation.

Bible Nurture and Reader Series

God Leads His People

Teacher's Manual

Grade 3

Rod and Staff Publishers, Inc.
P.O. Box 3, Hwy. 172
Crockett, Kentucky 41413
Telephone (606) 522-4348

BIBLE NURTURE AND READER SERIES

"If you train your children carefully until they are seven years old, they are already three-quarters educated." This quote recognizes the importance of the critical early years in molding a child's life. The influences of childhood become powerful, lasting impressions.

The type of schoolbooks used certainly affects the developing appetites of our children for reading material. We will not instill in them appreciation for godly values by feeding them frivolous nonsense. We hold the Bible to be the highest guide for life and the best source of training for our children. The Bible reveals God and His will. Proverbs 9:10 says, "The fear of the LORD is the beginning of wisdom: and the knowledge of the holy is understanding." It is important that our children are exposed to truth from the beginning of their learning experience.

For the student to be exposed to the truth of God's Word only in textbooks is not sufficient to give him the very best. It is necessary for the tutor, be he parent or other teacher, to be firmly rooted in the Word of God and have the power of God's presence in his life. The Bible must be treasured as God's message to mankind. On that conviction this series is built, with the Scriptures as its very substance.

This book is designed as part of a series and will be most effective if so used. The grade three material includes the following books.

Teacher's Manual

Pupil's Reader Units 1–3
Pupil's Reader Units 4, 5

Reading Workbook Unit 1
Reading Workbook Unit 2
Reading Workbook Unit 3
Reading Workbook Unit 4
Reading Workbook Unit 5

By
Rod and Staff Publishers, Inc.
Crockett, Kentucky 41413

Printed in U.S.A

ISBN 978-07399-0391-9

Catalog no. 11391.3

14 15 16 — 20 19 18 17 16

Table of Contents

A Word of Appreciation

It is with thanksgiving to God that we present these textbooks to those who are concerned about the spiritual welfare of their children. We believe that children are a heritage of the Lord and a sacred trust and that we dare not fail them in any area of their lives.

The *Bible Nurture and Reader Series* is possible only because of the work and leading of God in the lives of many faithful servants of His. We think first of all of our parents, ministers, and teachers who had a concern for us and faithfully taught and nurtured us in the Word of God. We appreciate those who have had a vision of the need for textbooks based on the Bible and who have given their encouragement and help in the writing and publishing of these books.

We appreciate the work of the author, Sister Lela Birky, who has a deep burden for Bible-based school texts to nurture children in the fear of God.

We want to give recognition to the fact that we have used ideas from many textbooks, workbooks, reference books, and other sources. We are grateful for the work of many teachers who have developed and shared valuable helps for teaching this series. Sister Amy Herr is the writer of the present revision of the workbooks and teacher's manual.

The Lord has provided strength in weakness, grace in trials, wisdom because we have none, joy in service, financial help, and faithful laborers in this work. May His Name receive honor and praise, and may we rejoice that we can be laborers together with Him.

Phonetic Symbols

/ā/	as in *pay*	/a/	as in *hat*
/ē/	as in *see*	/e/	as in *yes*
/ī/	as in *by*	/i/	as in *sit*
/ō/	as in *go*	/o/	as in *top*
/ū/	as in *cube*	/u/	as in *bug*
/o͞o/	as in *food*	/oo/	as in *foot*

/ou/	as in *out*	/sh/	as in *she*
/oi/	as in *boy*	/ch/	as in *chop*
/ô/	as in *saw*	/wh/	as in *when*
/ä/	as in *park*	/th/	as in *thin*
/ė/	as in *her*	/t͟h/	as in *that*
/ə/	the indefinite vowel sound heard in an unaccented syllable, representing any of the five vowels, as in a*lone*, *listen*, *flexible*, *consider*, su*ppose*	/ng/	as in *sing*
		/zh/	as in *measure*

To promote clear enunciation, many pronunciations are given with specific vowel sounds where a modern dictionary would use the schwa. There is limited usage of the schwa in this work to develop acquaintance with the symbol in preparation for using dictionaries and glossaries in other texts.

Unit One

Stories About David and Solomon

UNIT 1
General Plan

Lesson plans in this teacher's manual are divided into three sections. The heading of each section is listed below with an explanation of the general plan for that section.

I. Preparing to Read

New Words

The early lessons in this unit provide exercises to teach usage of the word lists and glossary at the back of the reader. Beyond these lessons, the children should habitually refer to the word list for their new lesson and look up the new words in the glossary. This may be a class activity in which you print the words on the board to drill pronunciations and discuss definitions.

In large class settings or for slow students it may be advisable to have the children read the lesson aloud at home each day to provide sufficient oral reading opportunity. The word study should then be done near the end of the day previous to the day the lesson is used in class.

The word study may be an individual activity in which each student assumes responsibility to look up the words himself before silent reading of the lesson. You can ensure a certain measure of attention to each word by assigning the list to be written with the pronunciation, part of speech, definition, or a sentence for each word.

Pointer Questions

To give purpose and to direct thought in silent reading, have the children consider a question or two before they read the story. These questions may be given in oral discussion and answered in discussion after reading.

Written on the board, the questions can become a standard guide to prepare the students for silent reading without attention from the teacher. The questions should then be answered in discussion following oral reading. You may have the children regularly write out answers to ensure each student's consideration of the questions.

Suggested pointer questions are provided in this part of the teacher's manual for each lesson.

II. Reader

Suggestions are given in the daily lesson plans to help establish proper posture and handling of the books as a routine standard. Pointers are also given to help develop expressive oral reading.

To help the children grow in comprehension skills, discuss the story content after oral reading. Lead them into inference reasoning and understanding of cause and effect.

Suggested discussion questions are provided in this part of the daily lesson plans.

III. Workbook

A common workbook activity is the exercise of writing sentences to answer questions. The children will need help to learn this skill. Discuss some of the questions and let the children give oral answers. Word their given answer in a sentence and have them repeat it. Before long the children should be able to word the answers in sentences themselves in oral discussion. Take time to discuss the written answers sometimes and have the children rewrite answers that are not complete sentences. Give this training without penalizing the reading grade for sentence structure. Require good sentences and work until the children use them, or adjust the assignment and let the children know that you are not expecting sentences. Shorter answers may be acceptable, but do not confuse the children by accepting them as sentences. When grading sentences allow two points for each answer—one for answer content and one for sentence structure.

Occasional pointers are given for other exercises, especially when new work is introduced.

Most lessons include a phonics activity to review the phonics learned in Grades One and Two. If some students have not had a phonics course and need more thorough review, they may benefit from the course *Developing Better Reading* which is available from Rod and Staff Publishers.

Answer Key

When sentence answers are called for, they are given with the key thought italicized. Wording may vary greatly but the children's answers should include the key thought.

If your schedule allows it, check the workbook lessons in class. Discuss sentence answers to help the children recognize sentences, but do not invite the frustration of trying to discuss every sentence for every child in a large class. Encourage the children to exercise some judgment in marking the sentences themselves, perhaps with a question mark for cases in which they cannot decide. Confirm or correct their judgment by checking that part of the lesson yourself later.

Checking and discussing the lesson in class can provide you with a more realistic evaluation of the children's ability and progress than the accumulation of percentages based on written work only. Use your personal evaluation as a basis for report card grades and blend it with recorded grades from occasional lessons. Recommended lessons for recording grades on the written work are noted in the answer key with the word *Gradebook* and number of points. The occasional oral quizzes provided in this manual may also be used as part of the total grade.

Before you distribute the workbooks, remove and file the unit test found on the last pages of each book.

Unit 1 Lessons

LESSON 1
David Mourns for Saul

I. Preparing to Read

Introduce the workbook and have the children do the exercise titled *Preparing to Read* found at the beginning of Lesson 1. You may choose to go over the exercise with the class and drill the pronunciation and meaning of the new words.

Explore the reader with the children, noting the table of contents, unit divisions, glossary, and word lists. Locate Lesson 1 of Unit 1 and discuss the title of the story. "What was the reason for mourning? Had David and Saul been close friends?" Assign the story to be read silently.

II. Reader

Teach the children the procedure you prefer for oral reading of the story. Having a particular place and posture helps foster attention to the reading. Have them file in an orderly way to an area where they can stand in a class line or sit around a class table, or have them stand by their desks in turn to read.

Teach the children to hold the readers in two hands, not on their hips or propped against their stomachs. Let one hand hold the book under the binding and the other rest on the open pages to steady the book. Page by putting a finger on the edge of a corner and pulling it toward you.

After oral reading, discuss the lesson content. Generally conduct this discussion with the books closed. On occasion you may have the children refer to the reader for particular information or to find certain words.

"Who was the first king? What kind of king was he? Who would be the next king?

"Where was David when Saul died? Why do you think he was not in Israel? [He had fled to escape Saul.] How did David find out about Saul's death? How did he feel about it? How did the messenger think he would feel? What did the messenger say that was not true? Why did he say it? What kind of reward do you think he expected? [perhaps praise, money, favored position in David's kingdom] What kind of reward did he receive? [death]"

Note:

There is a considerable amount of killing in these stories from the history of Israel. How should a Christian teacher relate to it?

First of all, recognize that the Bible gives these stories simply because they are true. They are accounts of real events as they actually happened. Second, godly men of Old Testament times sometimes dealt with evil by killing wicked people (as when Elijah killed the prophets of Baal). Since Jesus came, His true followers avoid such acts because He taught them to not resist evil by physical force.

Consider also that in Bible times, rulers were not appointed because they won elections. Some Israelite kings did rule as God's anointed; but when people did not recognize this, whoever proved himself the strongest (by fighting and killing his opponents) became the king. A king's sons and later descendants often ruled after him, but only if they also maintained power over their opponents. At any time, another man might rise up against the king, sometimes unsuccessfully (as Absalom against David) and sometimes successfully (as Jehu against Ahab). Some countries today are still ruled by whoever proves himself the strongest.

Explain these things in a simple way at appropriate times, without making a major point of it. This should help your students to see the killing in its proper perspective.

III. Workbook

Discuss the directions for the exercises in the workbook section *After You Read the Story.* Note that part C calls for sentence answers. To teach the children to word their answers in good sentences, work with them on sentence structure frequently, giving help in wording. When giving this assignment, illustrate the difference between a complete sentence and a fragment. Let the children give answers for some of the questions, and build sentences with their answers orally. They may automatically give sentence answers for "why" questions if you avoid using *because* to begin the answers.

If you have opportunity to correct and discuss the finished lesson with the class, suggest wording improvements for sentence fragments found then as well. Allow this to be a teaching time and do not be quick to lower grades because of incomplete sentences.

You may want to discuss some of the words the children listed in part D, and what the words mean.

ANSWER KEY

Preparing to Read

A. Amalekite, bracelet, continue, escaped, Gilboa

B.
1. a, a tribe of people from the wilderness of Sinai
2. b, band worn around the wrist or arm
3. b, keep on
4. a, got free; got away from danger
5. a, the mountain where Saul and Jonathan were slain

After You Read the Story

A.
1. bad
2. bad
3. good
4. good
5. good
6. bad

B.
1. a, b, e
2. b, c, d
3. a, c, e

C.
1. He had *taken his own way* instead of obeying God.
2. David was *not in the land of Israel* when they were killed.
3. He *thought David would be glad* that Saul was dead.

4. He knew that God wanted him to honor Saul as *God's anointed* one.
5. He knew it was a *very serious thing* to kill God's anointed king.
6. *God had always taken care* of David.

D. 2 Samuel 1:1-16
(Possible answers)

slaughter	whence
abode	anguish
rent	hither
obeisance	testified

(Other correct answers)

again	hath	slay	by	knowest	stranger
against	have	slew	chance	life	stretch
art	hold	smote	comest	likewise	sword
behold	house	stand	could	live	thee
blood	is	stood	day	lo	then
			days	matter	thine
			destroy	mourned	third
			earth	mouth	thou
			even	my	thy
			fall	near	two
			fasted	now	upon
			fled	pass	wast
			followed	pray	went
			forth	returned	when
			hand	saying	whole
			hard	slain	Ziklag

E. 1. king
2. way
3. kill
4. land
5. head
6. took
7. told

LESSON 2
David Anointed King Over Judah

I. Preparing to Read

Have the children do the exercise with the new words in the workbook. *Peaceably* is labeled as an adverb in the glossary, which may be an unfamiliar term to the children. If it raises a question, tell the children they will study that kind of word later in the year. A simple definition of adverbs as words that tell how something is done may be given.

Write the words on the board and drill their pronunciations.

Give purpose to the silent reading with these pointer questions.

1. Why was David in the Philistines' land?
2. Who was made king besides David?

II. Reader

Review your standards for oral reading class.

After oral reading, discuss the story.

"Who made the battle against Israel in which Saul and his sons were killed?

"Where was David when he heard about it? Why did David not decide for himself where to go then? [He knew it was not safe to be anywhere except where God wanted him to be.] Where did God want him to go? Was that where he had lived before when he was in the land of Israel?

"What was done to David at Hebron? Over how much of the kingdom did he rule? Who ruled over the rest of the tribes?"

Discuss the map in the workbook. Explain the four directions and how to tell in what direction a person would travel to go from one place to another. "What happened at Jabesh-gilead? What happened at Mount Gilboa? What river did the men of Jabesh-gilead cross when they went to get Saul's body to bury it? If you were at the Sea of Galilee and traveled toward the Dead Sea, what direction would you be going? If you were in the Philistines' land and went to Bethlehem, what direction would you be traveling? What direction would you travel from Gibeon to Mount Gilboa?

"What happened at Gibeon? What did Abner mean when he suggested having some of the men from each side play before them? [This was not a game. It was a contest in which the men would kill each other and the rest would look on as spectators.] How many men were in the contest? [twenty-four] What happened after that? Who won the battle?

"Tell the story of Abner and Asahel.

"Why did Joab and his brother give up chasing Abner?"

III. Workbook

Discuss again the formation of sentences for the answers in part C. Let the children say what the answers will be and have them construct oral sentences with their answers.

Review the four directions on the map and how to tell in what direction a person would travel to go from one place to another.

ANSWER KEY

Preparing to Read

A.

People	*Places*
Asahel	Hebron
Ish-bosheth	Jabesh
Joab	Jabesh-gilead

B. (Order interchangeable)

1. homeland—the country that is one's home
2. inheritance—something received from your parents or someone who died
3. peaceably—with peace; pleasantly
4. persuaded—urged and won over to do or believe
5. reigned—ruled

After You Read the Story

A.
1. Joab
2. Abner
3. Ish-bosheth
4. David
5. Asahel
6. David
7. Ish-bosheth
8. David

B.

Across	*Down*
1. fight	1. fourteen
5. go	2. Gad
6. pool	3. top
7. war	4. kill
9. deer	8. brother
11. anointed	10. old
12. twenty	11. after
13. Lord	

C. 1. *Saul* was Ish-bosheth's father.
2. Ish-bosheth reigned as king for *two years.*
3. Abner meant the men should *fight* each other.

D. 1. (seas and Jordan River colored blue)
2. Judah
3. Gad
4. (Philistines' land colored green)
5. (Judah colored yellow)
6. (Gad colored orange)
7. south (accept southwest)
8. east
9. north
10. west (accept northwest)

E. 1. Bethlehem
2. Hebron
3. Mount Gilboa
4. Jabesh-gilead
5. Gibeon

F. 1. fled
2. tribe
3. brave
4. tree
5. play
6. blew
7. still

LESSON 3
Abner Is Slain

I. Preparing to Read

You may wish to introduce the new word exercise in class and have the children practice orally making sentences with the words.

Pointer Questions to direct silent reading

1. What made Abner change sides?
2. Who on the other side did not accept him?

II. Reader

Review your posture standards and conduct oral reading class.

Discussion

"Who had the larger kingdom? Who had the stronger kingdom? Why? What made Abner change sides?

"What did Joab think of Abner's change? What can we find in the story to give us an idea whether Abner really meant to support David or if he was trying to deceive him? [He was angry with Ish-bosheth. He talked to the older men of Ish-bosheth's kingdom in David's favor, which he would hardly have done if he wanted to deceive David.]

"What did Joab do without David's command or knowledge? What did David think of it when he found it out?

"What did David do to make sure people would not think he had wanted Abner killed? Why would people think that he had wanted it? [A captain should be acting on his king's direction.]

"What did David call Abner?"

III. Workbook

Encourage the children again to write complete sentences in part B. Give suggestions for improvement when correcting the work and have the children rewrite incomplete sentences.

ANSWER KEY

Preparing to Read

A. accused, guilt, casket, sackcloth

B. (Individual sentences)

After You Read the Story

A.
1. no
2. yes
3. no
4. yes
5. no
6. no
7. no
8. no (review from Lesson 2)
9. no
10. no

B.
1. Abner had *killed* his brother *Asahel.*
2. David *followed the casket* to the grave and *wept.*
3. David told *Joab and everyone with him* to mourn for Abner.
4. David called Abner *a prince and a great man.*
5. *God would punish him.*

C.
1. group
2. stronger
3. kingdom
4. long
5. between
6. change
7. afraid
8. worked
9. kept
10. angry
11. given
12. another
13. also
14. messengers
15. wife
16. talked
17. older
18. tried
19. people
20. before
21. after
22. secret
23. smote
24. brother
25. aside
26. today
27. prince
28. great
29. punish
30. done

D. (Possible characters)

Abner—angry at accusation of Ish-bosheth

Ish-bosheth—fearful of Abner's threat

Michal's husband—sad to lose his wife

Joab—displeased at David's acceptance of Abner

David—displeased that Joab killed Abner

E.
1. son
2. him
3. will
4. sin
5. man
6. back
7. sad

LESSON 4
David Becomes King Over all Israel

I. Preparing to Read

Begin to establish a routine procedure for acquaintance with the new words. As a class activity, you may have the children say (or spell) the new words for you to write on the board. Then have the definition for each one given from the glossary. Discuss the meanings, use the words in sentences, and drill pronunciations.

Another method may be, as an individual study, to have the children habitually turn to the word list and look up each word in the glossary. You may want to have them write the words with definitions, pronunciations, parts of speech, or sentences to promote satisfactory consideration of each word.

Pointer Questions to guide silent reading

1. What did the two captains want in the king's house?
2. What had David done to get the kingdom for himself?

II. Reader

Let the children tell you what is expected in posture. Conduct oral reading class.

Discussion

"What effect did it have on Ish-bosheth's kingdom when Abner was killed? How did two of his other captains respond? What did the rest of the people do when their king was dead?

"Did David appreciate that Ish-bosheth was killed? What did he do to show his disapproval? What did he do that showed his respect for Ish-bosheth?

"How long had David been king before this? Where had he had the seat of his kingdom? Where did he want to have his palace now as king of all Israel? What problem did he have with those plans? Who helped him out?

"Who was Hiram? What did he do?

"How did it happen that David became king?

"How many sons did David have?"

III. Workbook

ANSWER KEY

A.
1. Carpenters
2. Messengers
3. Captains
4. Kings
5. Masons
6. Carpenters, masons

B.
1. messengers
2. masons
3. captains
4. carpenters
5. kings
6. carpenters, masons

C.
1. a
2. b
3. b
4. a
5. b
6. b
7. b

D.
1. Saul
2. bed
3 Abner
4. 7½
5. thirty-three
6. king
7. carpenters, masons
8. cedar
9. Six
10. eleven

E.
1. (Judah colored green)
2. (Manasseh, Benjamin, Naphtali, Reuben colored yellow)
3. (Dan, Gad, Zebulon, Simeon colored orange)
4. (Issachar, Ephraim, Asher colored red)
5. south
6. (*Jerusalem* circled)
7. (arrow from Hebron to Jerusalem)
8. (Dead Sea and Jordan River labeled)

F.
1. weak
2. came
3. grave
4. while
5. feed
6. made
7. wait

LESSON 5
David Brings the Ark to Jerusalem

I. Preparing to Read

Give direction, if needed, to establish the routine word study.

Pointer Questions

1. What did the Philistines take along to battle?
2. How many men went along to bring the ark to Jerusalem?

II. Reader

Let the children demonstrate proper posture before you proceed with oral reading. This should become habit so the need to mention it daily can fade.

Check comprehension with an oral quiz. Have the children write the answers to these true and false questions.

1. The Philistines came to fight against David. (T)
2. The battle was in a wheat field. (F)
3. David asked the Lord what to do. (T)
4. God promised to deliver the Philistines into his hands. (T)
5. The Philistines took idols along to battle. (T)
6. The idols helped the Philistines win. (F)

7. David and his men kept the idols they found. (F)
8. The Philistines came for the second battle. (T)
9. This time they fought by the mulberry trees. (T)
10. There were many battles with the Philistines. (T)
11. The ark was still in the land of the Philistines. (F)
12. Samuel was still living at this time. (F)
13. David wanted to bring the ark to Hebron. (F)
14. Thirty thousand men went with David to get the ark. (T)
15. They put the ark on a cart pulled by donkeys. (F)
16. Uzzah touched the ark because it was dirty. (F)
17. Uzzah died because he touched the ark. (T)
18. The ark stayed at Obed-edom's house six months. (F)
19. The priests carried the ark on their shoulders with staves. (T)
20. The ark was put in a tent at Jerusalem. (T)

Discussion

Discuss the sentence "The Lord . . . blessed the house of Obed-edom because of the ark of God." Did God bless the floors and walls and roof of the place where Obed-edom lived? *House* here refers to the household, or people and affairs of his family.

III. Workbook

Give some attention to sentence structure for the answers in part B before and after the children do the work.

ANSWER KEY

A.

3	6	8	10
2	4	7	11
1	5	9	12

B.
1. David wanted to bring the ark to *Jerusalem.*
2. Only the *priests* were to carry the ark.
3. It was to be carried with *staves.*
4. He *died.*
5. He wanted to *steady* the ark.
6. The ark would be put in a *tent.*
7. It stayed with them *three months.*

C.

1. a	13. b
2. c	14. a
3. b	15. c
4. c	16. b
5. b	17. a
6. a	18. c
7. b	19. c
8. a	20. b
9. c	21. a
10. b	22. c
11. a	23. b
12. c	24. a

D. (General idea)

David wanted water from the well at Bethlehem, so three men broke through the Philistines and got some for him. But he did not drink it because the men had risked their lives for it. He poured it out to the Lord.

E. 1. him
2. full
3. left
4. back
5. ox
6. put
7. last

LESSON 6
God Makes Great Promises to David

I. Preparing to Read

Pointer Questions

1. Why did God not want David to build His house?
2. What did God say He would make for David?

II. Reader

Discussion

"About what was David not satisfied? What pleased God about David's desire? What did not please God? How did David find out what God thought? Who did God want to build His house?

"How many reasons can you find for not building a house for God? [He had never had one before. He had never told them that He wanted a house.]

"What kind of house did God make for David? [*House* in this sentence means "family."] How is God making David's kingdom stand forever?

"How did David feel about the things God said? What did he do because he felt so thankful?"

III. Workbook

ANSWER KEY

A. 1. when
2. where
3. where
4. when
5. when
6. when
7. when
8. where
9. when
10. where
11. where

B. 1. It did not seem right that *he had a nice cedar house* while the ark was in a tent.
2. David had been a *man of war.*
3. *David's son* would build God's house.
4. God gave David a *family.*
5. *Jesus* came from David's family, and He will reign forever.

C. 1. peacemaker
2. peaceful
3. peacefully
4. peace
5. pleased
6. displeased
7. pleasing
8. please
9. lovely
10. loved
11. loves
12. loving
13. thanks
14. thankful
15. thankless
16. thanked

17. promise
18. promising
19. promised
20. served
21. servant
22. serve
23. especially
24. special

D. five

E. 1. Na ***th*** an
2. ***th*** is
3. ***ch*** ildren
4. ***th*** ere
5. wi ***th***
6. ***wh*** o
7. ***th*** ought
8. ***th*** eir
9. ***sh*** ould
10. ***sh*** own
11. ***th*** ings
12. ***th*** ankful
13. ***th*** at (or) ***wh*** at
14. ***wh*** at (or) ***th*** at
15. ***sh*** all
16. ***th*** ese

LESSON 7
David Shows Kindness to Others

I. Preparing to Read

Pointer Questions

1. Why did David want to find someone from Saul's house?
2. Why could not Mephibosheth work for David as other servants?

II. Reader

Keep prompting the class for correct posture and handling of the book in oral reading class until it is habitual.

Discussion

"Who was Jonathan?
"Who was Ziba?
"Who was Mephibosheth?
"Who was Hanun?"

Have the class find the land of the children of Ammon on the map. Find Jericho and let the children tell what happened there. Observe that the Jordan River had to be crossed to get to Hanun's land.

III. Workbook

In part D, the antonym for the second sentence of each number may be found in Lesson 7 in the reader.

ANSWER KEY

A. 1. good
2. good
3. good
4. good
5. good
6. bad
7. bad
8. good

B. 1. Jonathan
2. Ziba
3. Mephibosheth
4. Ziba
5. Mephibosheth
6. Jonathan
7. Saul
8. Hanun
9. David
10. Hanun

C.
1. (Ammon colored purple)
2. (Israel colored yellow)
3. (*Jerusalem* circled)
4. (*Jericho* underlined)
5. Jordan
6. yes
7. east
8. west
9. (Bethlehem labeled)
10. (Hebron labeled—south of Bethlehem)

D.
1. a. forgot b. remembered
2. a. meanness b. kindness
3. a. dead b. alive
4. a. master b. servant
5. a. young b. old
6. a. brave b. afraid
7. a. daughter b. son

(2 points for each number)

E. (Suffixes are to be circled.)
1. ful, thank
2. ness, kind
3. ed, want
4. ed, answer
5. s, crop
6. ing, honor
7. ly, great
8. ly, exact
9. ed, treat
10. ful, shame
11. ly, hard
12. s, son
13. ing, send
14. s, servant
15. ed, kill
16. ly, kind
17. ed, command
18. ly, sure
19. ed, bow
20. ed, look

(2 points for each number)

Gradebook: 82 points

LESSON 8
David Displeases God

I. Preparing to Read

Pointer Questions

1. Why did Joab divide his army into two groups?
2. Which commandments did David break?

II. Reader

When maintaining class posture requires less concentration, give attention to the quality of oral reading. Point out punctuation marks and demonstrate appropriate pauses between sentences. Demonstrate the effect of grouping words in phrases versus word-by-word reading. Practice recognition of good phrase grouping.

Discussion

"Why do you think the children of Ammon decided to fight Israel? [They probably expected Israel to fight them and thought they would have a better chance of winning if they got help and attacked Israel, rather than being attacked sometime when they were not prepared.]

"What did Joab do when he realized that two armies had come to fight? How do you know Joab was depending on God in the battle? [In planning the battle he told his brother, "The Lord will do whatever seems good to Him."]

"Which nation had many of its people killed?

"Who decided to make the next battle? What did he do while his army went to fight? Where was David when he saw a beautiful woman? Why do you think he was up on the roof? [Discuss cultural differences.]

"What wicked thing did David do?

"Who killed Uriah? [The soldiers of the city Israel attacked killed him, but in a sense we can say David killed him because David purposely required the arrangement to bring about his death.] Who was glad that Uriah was dead? Who was sad?

"What did David do when Bath-sheba was finished mourning? Was everything all right then? [No, David had committed great sin, and even though people did not know about it, his sin mattered very much.]"

III. Workbook

Discuss some of the word relations in part B and do a few samples with the class.

Practice orally some phrase reading from part C. If the children do not seem to have a sense of what sounds right, it may help to tell them that a sentence generally sounds best when the words are grouped so that the phrases end with a noun or a verb.

ANSWER KEY

A. (Accept reasonable variations.)

1. fight
2. Syrians
3. Joab
4. front
5. behind
6. brother
7. afraid
8. ran
9. Ammon
10. Joab
11. Jerusalem
12. evening
13. roof
14. beautiful
15. Uriah
16. covet
17. adultery
18. kill
19. killed
20. wife
21. Joab
22. front
23. hottest
24. himself
25. killed
26. city
27. brave
28. Israel
29. husband
30. David
31. his
32. son
33. displeased

B.

1. Bethlehem (The rest are people.)
2. five (The rest relate to God's laws.)
3. joy (The rest name the time of day.)
4. brave (The rest are synonyms.)
5. delight (The rest have an unpleasant connotation.)
6. water (The rest relate to buildings.)
7. agree (The rest relate to war.)
8. servant (The rest name blood relatives.)
9. obey (The rest are wicked acts.)

10. repeat (The rest imply destruction.)
11. sneaked (The rest name manner of looking.)
12. encounter (The rest are derivatives of *courage*.)
13. beginning (The rest refer to ending.)
14. spoon (The rest rhyme.)
15. carrot (The rest name geographical features.)
16. alone (The rest are associated with written communication.)
17. no (The rest are pronouns.)
18. Israel (The rest name positions.)
19. love (The rest describe appearance.)
20. hot (The rest have the suffix *–est*.)
21. also (The rest name relation in position.)

C.
1. a
2. b
3. b
4. b
5. b
6. a
7. a
8. b
9. a
10. b
11. b
12. b

D. (Prefixes are to be circled.)

1.	dis,	please
2.	be,	cause
3.	un,	happy
4.	re,	make
5.	de,	part
6.	re,	turn
7.	pre,	view
8.	de,	grade
9.	un,	real
10.	dis,	favor
11.	un,	true
12.	be,	came
13.	dis,	obey
14.	pre,	pay
15.	de,	throne
16.	un,	rest
17.	be,	long
18.	de,	face
19.	pre,	caution
20.	be,	moan

LESSON 9
"You Are the Man"

I. Preparing to Read

Pointer Questions

1. Why did Nathan tell David a story?
2. Who would find out about David's secret sin?

II. Reader

Write these sentences from the story on the board and discuss the punctuation and appropriate expression.

What a shock this must have been for David!

How could he be that cruel rich man?

Encourage the children to observe punctuation and group words in phrases as they read.

Discussion

"Tell about the poor man's lamb. What happened to the lamb? Why?

"What did David think should be done about the rich man's cruelty?

"Why did Nathan tell that story? [to show David how cruel his own sin was] How did Nathan know about David's sin? [God told him.]

"How was David like the rich man in the story?

"Who did Nathan say had killed Uriah?

"Would David die for his cruelty as he said the man in the story should? What would happen because of his sin? Which of those things would be the worst? [Occasion for God's enemies to speak evil is more far-reaching than the death of one child or the suffering of one man or his family.]"

III. Workbook

Prepare the children to make proper judgment in question 6 of part A if you have not covered the last part of the reader discussion above.

Part B presents an outline of the story. Point out that an outline of a picture lets you see the picture without showing a lot of details. An outline of a story does that as well. Discuss the outline with the children, pointing out the main headings, then noting that the lettered points under each heading all give more details about that heading.

ANSWER KEY

A.
1. b
2. a
3. c
4. c
5. b
6. a
7. b

B.
I. A. ewe lamb
   B. him and his children
   C. of his own food
   D. of his cup
   E. in his lap
   F. a daughter to him

II. A. his own animal
   B. the poor man's only lamb

III. A. die
   B. four lambs

IV. A. king over Israel
   B. him from Saul
   C. his master's house and wives
   D. the house of Israel and Judah
   E. given him more

V. A. Uriah
   B. Uriah's wife

VI. A. God's enemies to speak evil
   B. would die
   C. suffer
   D. would suffer
   E. depart from David's house

C.
1. flocks
2. herds
3. lamb
4. instead
5. depart
6. rich
7. secretly
8. great
9. cause
10. delivered
11. wicked
12. animal
13. meal
14. cruel
15. angry

D.
1. many
2. together
3. poor
4. little
5. die
6. cruel
7. wife
8. daughter
9. man
10. punish

E. 1. prophet
2. ewe
3. four
4. herd
5. to
6. would
7. be
8. great
9. read
10. one

LESSON 10
David Suffers for His Sin

I. Preparing to Read

Pointer Questions

1. What made David think his child had died?
2. Why did David act differently after his child died?

II. Reader

Write these sentences on the board and practice expressive reading.

What might he do to himself when he heard that the child was dead?

"Can I bring him back again?"

Discussion

"Why did the child get sick? What did David do? Why? How long did David go without eating?

"Why were the servants afraid to tell David his child was dead? Can you imagine what they thought he might do? [Perhaps he would lose his sanity or do himself some physical harm or starve himself.]

"What made David realize that the child was dead? What did he do that surprised the servants?

"David said he would go to the child but the child would not return to him. Where would he go to be with the child? When would that be?

"Who was Solomon? What does *Solomon* mean?"

III. Workbook

For part D, review the definition of *synonym* as given in Lesson 9. If the children need help to understand the sentences, let them refer to the previous lessons which the sentences review.

ANSWER KEY

A. 1. a. message
b. ground
c. face
d. clothes
e. food

2. a. sick
b. God's
c. older
d. seventh
e. sad

3. a. prayed
b. whispered
c. comforted
d. died
e. worshiped

B. 1. a. when his child became sick.
b. after their son died.
c. after he was dead.
2. a. upon the ground.
b. to the house of God.
c. on this earth.

C. 1. David would not *get up* or *eat.*
2. They *did not know what he might do* to himself.
3. He saw the servants *whispering.*
4. (Any five of these)
He *got up* from the earth.
He *washed his face.*
He *changed his clothes.*
He *went to the house of God.*
He *worshiped the Lord.*
He *ate.*
5. David would go to the child *when he died.*
6. The Lord gave them *other sons.*
7. Solomon means *"peaceable and perfect."*

D. 1. torn
2. honor
3. mourned
4. asked
5. deer
6. became
7. angry
8. agreement
9. casket
10. killed
11. carry
12. died
13. build
14. belonged
15. clothes
16. wait
17. speak evil of God

E. 1. asked, t
2. acted, ed
3. looked, t
4. fasted, ed
5. answered, d
6. worshiped, t
7. prayed, d
8. washed, t
9. comforted, ed
10. whispered, d

LESSON 11
Wicked Absalom

I. Preparing to Read

Pointer Questions

1. For what did Absalom beg his father?
2. What false news did David hear?

II. Reader

Have the children find quotation marks in the lesson and discuss the feeling and tones of the speakers. Encourage the children to try to show that feeling in their reading.

Test comprehension with this oral quiz. Have the children write *true* or *false* to answer each question.

1. David had many sons. (T)
2. Absalom and Amnon were half brothers. (T)
3. Amnon wanted to kill Absalom. (F)
4. Sheepshearers butcher sheep. (F)
5. Absalom invited his brothers to come to where his sheepshearers were. (T)
6. Absalom wanted David and his servants to come too. (T)
7. David blessed Absalom. (T)
8. King David went with Absalom. (F)
9. All the kings sons went with Absalom. (T)
10. Absalom's servants killed Amnon. (T)
11. Amnon was killed before the rest of the king's sons came. (F)
12. The rest of the sons rode away on camels. (F)
13. David believed that his sons were all killed. (T)
14. David lay down on his bed in grief. (F)
15. David's servants tore their clothes. (T)
16. David's uncle told David that only Amnon was killed. (F)
17. Absalom fled to another country. (T)
18. Absalom came back after two years. (F)
19. Absalom lived at Jerusalem three years without seeing his father. (F)
20. Joab willingly came when Absalom called for him. (F)

III. Workbook

In part D do a few examples with the class.

ANSWER KEY

A.
1. b
2. c
3. b
4. a
5. c

B.
1. Someone told him *all the king's sons were slain.*
2. *David's nephew* had a true message.
3. He could show David the *king's sons coming.*
4. Absalom had *killed Amnon.*
5. David longed *to see Absalom* again.

C.
1. three years
2. two years
3. five years

D.
1. prince
2. princess
3. Jew, Jewess
4. prophet, prophetess
5. servant, master, handmaid, mistress
6. husband, wife
7. uncle, nephew, aunt, niece
8. wizard, witch

E.
1. sheep shearer
2. watch man
3. some one
4. hill side
5. house hold
6. every thing

7. hair cut
8. what ever
9. hand maid
10. grand child

LESSON 12
Absalom Deceives His Father and the People

I. Preparing to Read

Pointer Questions

1. Why did Joab go to Absalom?
2. Why did Absalom want to go to Hebron?

II. Reader

Consider the quotations and their expression again.

Discussion

"How often had Absalom called for Joab without getting a response? Why do you think Joab did not come? [perhaps because of disapproval of Absalom because he had killed Amnon] What did Absalom do that brought Joab? What did Absalom want with Joab?

"Was David ready to receive Absalom again? How did he show how he felt?

"How much hair did Absalom cut off each year?

"What made the people like Absalom?

"What did Absalom say he wanted to do at Hebron? What did he really want to do? How many men did he take along from Jerusalem? Did they know why Absalom was taking them?

"Who was the wise man Absalom sent for?"

III. Workbook

A short cut for part C would be to give only the number of the commandment for each answer.

ANSWER KEY

A. 1. *Absalom's servants* set Joab's field on fire.
2. *David kissed Absalom.*
3. Absalom got a haircut *once a year.*
4. Absalom wanted to be *king.*
5. Absalom *kissed* them and *said nice words* to them.
6. He wanted *to be made king.*
7. Absalom had a *handsome* face.
8. He had a *wicked* heart.

B.
1. no
2. no
3. yes
4. no
5. yes
6. no
7. yes

C.
a. (8) "Thou shalt not steal."
b. (5) "Honour thy father and thy mother."
c. (9) "Thou shalt not bear false witness."
d. (6) "Thou shalt not kill."
e. (10) "Thou shalt not covet."
f. (1) "Thou shalt have no other gods before me."

D.
1. beautiful
2. strong
3. healthy
4. heavy
5. kind
6. wise
7. wicked
8. run
9. early
10. right
11. follow
12. pleased

E. (Bold letters are to be circled.)
1. time ***s*** z
2. Ab ***s*** alom s
3. word ***s*** z
4. ***s*** ide s
5. in ***s*** tead s
6. Joab' ***s*** z
7. promi ***s*** e s
8. ha ***s*** z
9. plea ***s*** ed z
10. ***s*** ound s
11. ***s*** et s
12. the ***s*** e z
13. ***s*** oon s
14. hou ***s*** e s
15. a ***s*** ked s
16. becau ***s*** e z
17. ***s*** ent s
18. ***s*** aid s
19. ***s*** erve s
20. rea ***s*** on z
21. him ***s*** elf s
22. wa ***s*** z
23. mo ***s*** t s
24. I ***s*** rael z
25. ***s*** trong s
26. an ***s*** wered s
27. ***s*** even s
28. pound ***s*** z
29. tribe ***s*** z
30. wi ***s*** e z
31. hand ***s*** ome s
32. out ***s*** ide s
33. thought ***s*** s
34. ***s*** tand s
35. be ***s*** ide s
36. problem ***s*** z
37. Jeru ***s*** alem s
38. ***s*** ay s
39. li ***s*** ten s
40. ***s*** peak s

LESSON 13
David Flees From Absalom

I. Preparing to Read

Pointer Questions

1. Why would it be dangerous for David to stay at Jerusalem?
2. From where had Ittai come and why?

II. Reader

Discuss the feelings of the people in the story and challenge your students to read in a way that will express that feeling.

Discussion

"How did David find out about the danger? Why was he in a hurry to leave Jerusalem? Who did not go along? Who were the six hundred men who went with David? Why had they come to David? [They came to him because they had troubles.]

"Which way did they go from Jerusalem? [Follow their move on the map in Lesson 16 in the workbook.]

"Who took the ark back to Jerusalem?

"Did David know whether he would come back again? What do you think were some of the possibilities in his mind when he said, 'Let Him do to me whatever He sees is good'? [Perhaps God would allow death or banishment as punishment for something David had done that displeased Him.]

"How would David discover whether God was pleased with him? [He would wait in the wilderness to hear from Zadok and see what happened.]"

III. Workbook

Discuss some samples for exercises in parts D and E. Have the children note that the *–er* form of the word drops the *s*.

ANSWER KEY

A.

2	5	10
1	6	9
3	8	12
4	7	11

B.

1. They said, "We are *ready to do whatever you choose* to do."
2. He said, "*Hurry,* or he will come upon us suddenly."
3. Ittai had come to David only *the day before.*
4. He would stay *until he heard* from Zadok.
5. David and his men were *weeping.*
6. David took Ahithophel's advice as *advice from God.*
7. He was afraid Ahithophel would *give advice against him.*
8. David *prayed* that God would turn Ahithophel's advice into foolishness.

C.

1. ~~new~~, knew
2. ~~hisself~~, himself
3. ~~came~~, come

4. ~~Wee~~, We
5. ~~strayed~~, stayed
6. ~~ahed~~, ahead
7. ~~stangers~~, strangers
8. ~~befoe~~, before
9. ~~bake~~, back
10. ~~tooth~~, truth
11. ~~write~~, right
12. ~~litte~~, little
13. ~~book~~, brook
14. ~~tarry~~, carry
15. ~~man~~, men
16. ~~peeping~~, weeping
17. ~~verily~~, very
18. ~~sinned~~, seemed
19. ~~feeled~~, felt
20. ~~among~~, along
21. ~~weed~~, would
22. ~~praised~~, prayed
23. ~~avdice~~, advice

D. 1. stranger
2. rider
3. ruler
4. singer
5. batter
6. messenger

E. 1. farmer
2. painter
3. gardener
4. seeker
5. climber
6. dreamer
7. grinder
8. pretender

Gradebook: 57 points
(One point for each number)

LESSON 14
David Hides

I. Preparing to Read

Pointer Questions

1. What did it mean for a person to have his clothes torn and to have ground on his head?
2. Why did David want to know what Absalom and his men were planning?

II. Reader

In oral reading, promote awareness of pronunciation. Encourage carefulness in saying the words completely and correctly. Practice saying the names in the story carefully.

Discussion

"Where did David worship the Lord? Why did he worship the Lord at a time like this? [God was still the same wonderful, mighty, loving Lord. Though David did not understand everything that God allowed, he knew that God was still worthy of praise.]

"How could Hushai best help David?

"How did Ziba help David?

"What did Ziba do that did not help David? [gave him a discouraging report about Mephibosheth]

"Did Shimei help or hinder David? How? What did Joab's brother call him? Why did he call him that? Was Shimei dead? [*Dead dog* was a term of contempt used to compare a man with something very much despised and worthless.]

"What did David think the Lord might do because of the cursing of Shimei? [He might give David blessings to make up for it.]"

III. Workbook

Review the principles of outlines. Point out that on this outline the main points are not sentences and the lettered points are not expected to be sentences either. Each item begins with a capital letter, however.

Give special attention to the directions for part B, doing a sample with the class.

ANSWER KEY

A. I. A. to be Absalom's friend
B. following Ahithophel's advice
C. what he heard in the king's house

II. A. Two donkeys
B. Two hundred loaves of bread
C. A hundred bunches of raisins
D. A hundred summer fruits
E. A bottle of wine

III. A. the king's family to ride on
B. the young men to eat
C. those who might become faint

IV. A. Cursed David
B. Threw stones and dust

B. 1. At last David reached the (top) of Mount Olivet, a mountain just a little east of Jerusalem.

2. While David was (on Mount Olivet,) Hushai, one of David's friends, came to meet him.

3. As Shimei cursed, he also threw (stones and dust) at King David and at all his servants.

4. Joab's brother said to David, "Why should this dead dog curse (my lord, the king?")

5. At last the king and all the people with him came to a place where they could (rest) themselves.

C.

1. b
2. b
3. a
4. b
5. b
6. a

7. b
8. b
9. a
10. b
11. a
12. a

D. Ahithophel, Mephibosheth

1. ne ***ph*** ew
2. ***ph*** easant
3. pro ***ph*** ecy
4. tele ***ph*** one
5. ele ***ph*** ant
6. pro ***ph*** et
7. ***ph*** lox
8. ***ph*** rase
9. gra ***ph***
10. or ***ph*** an
11. paragra ***ph***
12. ***ph*** onics
13. ***ph*** arise
14. ***ph*** ysician

LESSON 15
Hushai Helps David

I. Preparing to Read

Pointer Questions

1. What reason did Hushai give Absalom for being on his side?
2. Whose advice did Absalom prefer?

II. Reader

Emphasize careful pronunciation in oral reading again.

Discussion

"How did Husahi greet Absalom?

"Whom did Absalom mean when he referred to Hushai's friend?

"Why did Hushai say he would stay with Absalom? Whom had the Lord chosen to be king?

"What advice did Ahithophel give? What did Hushai say was not good about that advice? What was the real reason he did not want them to go that night?

"What did Hushai say they should do?

"Whose description of David was more nearly correct?

"Whose advice was followed? Why did they choose that?"

III. Workbook

Do some oral review with the class in preparation for part D.

ANSWER KEY

A.
1. A
2. H
3. H
4. H
5. H
6. A
7. A
8. H
9. A
10. H

B.
1. A
2. A
3. H
4. A
5. A
6. H
7. H
8. H

C.
1. water
2. arrow
3. deer
4. lion
5. bear
6. bees
7. fuel
8. snow
9. heavens
10. sea
11. dew
12. sand
13. bear
14. lion
15. sand
16. dew
17. deer
18. arrow
19. bees
20. heavens
21. sea
22. snow
23. fuel
24. water

D.
1. true
2. false
3. false
4. false
5. false
6. false
7. false
8. true
9. true
10. false
11. false
12. true
13. false
14. true
15. true
16. false
17. false
18. false
19. false
20. true
21. true
22. false
23. true
24. false
25. false
26. false
27. false
28. true
29. true
30. true
31. true
32. true
33. false
34. true
35. false
36. false
37. false
38. false

LESSON 16
Absalom Goes After David

I. Preparing to Read

Pointer Questions

1. To how many people was the message passed to get from Hushai to David?
2. What was the message?

II. Reader

Take an occasional grade on oral reading and continue to work on details of the areas that need improvement. A method for grading oral reading is described below.

Oral Reading Grades

Base the grade on the consideration of these five qualities:

1. Volume—Can the reading be heard across the room?
2. Smoothness—Are the words grouped in meaningful phrases, or does the reader pause to decode words?
3. Inflection—Does the rise and fall of tones convey appropriate expression?

4. Enunciation—Are the words pronounced clearly and correctly?
5. Correctness—Is the passage read as written, without skipping or adding words?

Evaluate performance in each area on a scale from 5–10, letting 10 represent the highest quality. Figure the total points as a percentage of 50. A child who performs excellently in all five areas would be graded 50/50 or 100%. Someone who rated an 8 in volume and a 10 in all the other areas would receive 48/50 or 96%. One given the ratings of 10, 8, 7, 9, and 8 in the five areas would total 42/50 or 84%.

At the end of the marking period let the oral reading average represent one-fourth of the total reading grade.

Discussion

"To whom did Hushai report the advice that was given?

"To whom did the priests tell the message? Why was the message given to her?

"To whom did the woman servant tell the message?

"What interrupted the priests' sons on their way to give David the message? Why was it unsafe to continue on their journey? [Absalom would send men to stop them and possibly kill them so David would not get their message.] Where did the priests' sons hide? Do you think the well had a wall around it? [probably not if it looked like the covering and corn were on the ground] Do you think the well had water in it? [not deep water if there was any]

"Did the priests' sons get the message to David? What time of day was it when they got there? Did the people wait till morning to respond to the message?

"Where did they go on the other side of the Jordan River? In what land were they? [Gilead. Discuss the workbook map with the children.] Who came to help David in the land of Gilead? What did they do to help? One of those men was from the land of Ammon, and one was from the land of Gilead.

"What happened to Ahithophel? Why?

"What did Absalom do in preparation to go after David? Who was Amasa? [Joab and Amasa were also cousins to Absalom.] Where did Absalom's men camp?

"How many captains did David have? Who were they?

"Why did the people not want David to go along to battle? [He was the king, and his life mattered so much more than any of the others, that they said he was worth ten thousand of them.]

"What did David command his captains? Why do you think he said that? [He loved his son Absalom.]"

III. Workbook

ANSWER KEY

A. 1. the priest's sons
2. a young boy
3. a woman
4. a well
5. a covering and ground corn
6. three
7. no
8. ten thousand

B. 1. He was disappointed because *Absalom did not follow his advice.*
2. *"Deal gently with Absalom for my sake."*

C. 1. b
2. d
3. a
4. c

D. (Commas in number 1 are to be circled.)
1. Some men took pity on David and brought beds, basins, dishes, wheat, barley, corn, beans, flour, honey, butter, cheese, sheep, and other things.
2. David's wives, sons, daughters, and servants fled from Jerusalem.
3. David and his company were hungry, thirsty, and tired.
4. David made Joab, Abishai, and Ittai captains.
5. Men from Rabbath-ammon, Lo-debar, and Rogelim brought things to David.
6. Amasa, Joab, and Absalom were all cousins.

E. 1. (directions *EAST, SOUTH,* and *WEST* printed in place)
2. east (or southeast)
3. (brown spot in area of Wilderness of Judah)
4. east (or northeast)
5. (dot in land of Gilead)
6. (green spot near dot for number 5)
7. (arrow from Rabbath-ammon to dot for number 5)

Gradebook: 27 points
(One point for each number)

LESSON 17
A Great Battle

I. Preparing to Read

Pointer Questions

1. What killed most of the people in the battle?
2. How did Cushi tell David that Absalom was dead?

II. Reader

Discussion

"How many of Absalom's men died in battle? How do you suppose the woods could kill the people? [As Absalom was caught, so others could have been caught in a way that killed them. Perhaps in fleeing, some fell and hit their heads or broke their necks. Thorn thickets may have caught and killed some who rode frantic animals.]

"What did Joab do that David did not want him to do? Do you think he had forgotten David's command? [One of the men reminded him of it just before he and his servants killed Absalom.] What did they do with Absalom's body?

"Do you remember another time that Joab killed a man against David's wishes? [He killed Abner.]

"Whom did Joab want to send to David with the news? Why do you think he did not want Zadok's son to go? [Joab said he should not go that day because the king's son was dead. When David knew Zadok's son was coming, he was sure there was good news. Perhaps Joab thought the news of Absalom's death was not a suitable message to be sent with the priest's son.]

"Did Zadok's son tell David that Absalom was dead? Did he know it? [Joab had said it when he refused to send him.] How did Zadok's son evade David's question?

"How did Cushi answer the question?

"How did David take the news?"

III. Workbook

ANSWER KEY

A.
1. a. that day.
   b. today.
   c. before Cushi
2. a. between the two gates of the city.
   b. above him on the roof over the wall.
   c. aside.
   d. to his room over the gate.
3. a. by the woods.
   b. faster than Cushi.
   c. alone.
   d. grieved.

B.
1. no
2. "I saw a commotion, but I did not know what it was all about."
3. yes
4. Joab had told him the king's son was dead.

C.
1. Absalom
2. Cushi
3. trumpet
4. pit
5. roof
6. gate
7. commotion
8. sword
9. wall
10. gatekeeper

D.
1. later, now
2. now, later
3. now, later
4. later, now

E.
1. Joab
2 Absalom
3. David
4. tree
5. pit
6. silver

F.
1. you
15. profit

F.

1. you
2. bows
3. soared
4. flower
5. grate
6. there
7. herd
8. rained
9. wore
10. piece
11. prints
12. threw
13. write
14. cent
15. profit
16. morning
17. sun
18. meet
19. rays
20. sow
21. too
22. soul
23. hare
24. no
25. buy
26. week
27. here
28. sum

LESSON 18
David Returns to Jerusalem

I. Preparing to Read

Pointer Questions

1. What made the people's joy turn to sorrow?
2. What did David do to Joab because of his disobedience?

II. Reader

Discussion

"Why were the people rejoicing? What destroyed their happiness? How did the people act then?

"What did Joab think of the way David was acting? What did he say to David? Did David do what Joab said he should?

"Why did David make a new captain? Who was it?

"Which was the last tribe to welcome David back to be their king?

"Who came to help David at the river?

"What did David want to do for Barzillai? Why did Barzillai refuse? Who went instead of Barzillai?

"How did David get across the river?"

III. Workbook

Do the first section of part D with the class.

ANSWER KEY

A.

1. c
2. a
3. a
4. b
5. b
6. a
7. b
8. a

B.

1. They were happy that God had given them the *victory* over their enemies.
2. When they heard that

David was weeping, they were sad.
3. *None of David's people would stay* with David that night.
4. He was displeased that *David was weeping* for Absalom.
5. He was displeased that *Absalom was killed.*

C.
2. B; top of his house
3. N; airplane
4. B; raisins, figs, dried corn
5. N; innerspring mattress
6. N; chocolate candy
7. B; sepulchre
8. N; cemetery
9. B; sackcloth and ashes
10. N; secretary, type
11. B; burnt offerings
12. B; ark of God
13. B; prophet
14. B; once a year
15. N; every month
16. B; priest
17. N; New Testament

D.
1. b
2. a
3. c
4. b
5. c
6. a
7. a
8. b
9. b
10. a
11. a
12. b
13. c
14. a
15. b
16. b
17. a
18. c

E.
1. joy, mourning
2. love, hate / enemies, friends
3. living, died
4. arose, sat
5. first, last
6. asked, told
7. won, lost
8. father, son
9. servants, king
10. coldly, warmly
11. east, west
12. rich, poor
13. little, much
14. good, bad
15. men, women

LESSON 19
The Tribes Quarrel

I. Preparing to Read

Pointer Questions

1. Why did Judah think they had more right to David?
2. Why did Israel think they had more right to David?

II. Reader

Discussion

"What was the sin that Shimei confessed?

"What did Abishai think should be done to Shimei? What did David say?

"Why had Mephibosheth not gone with David? [His servant deceived him, perhaps leaving when Mephibosheth waited for his donkey to be saddled.]

"Why did David say Ziba and Mephibosheth should divide the land? [He had earlier given it all to Mephibosheth. Then when he thought Mephibosheth was unfaithful, he promised it all to Ziba.] How did they settle the question of the land?

"Why did the tribes quarrel? Who do you think had more right to David? [Contrast Mephibosheth's attitude. He was not worried about his rights.]

"Which side had fiercer words?

"What came of the quarrel? Do you think Sheba will be a king?"

III. Workbook

ANSWER KEY

A.

1. Shimei
2. sinned
3. death
4. cursed
5. forgive
6. Jerusalem
7. feet
8. beard
9. clothes
10. donkey
11. deceived
12. untruth
13. Judah
14. trouble
15. Judah
16. Israel
17. related
18. ten
19. ten
20. Judah
21. Israel
22. Belial
23. Benjamin
24. Sheba
25. trumpet
26. Israel
27. Sheba
28. David

B. (One point for each answer)

1. a. f
   b. w
   c. f
2. a. w
   b. f
   c. w
3. a. f
   b. f
   c. w
4. a. f
   b. w
   c. f

C. (Two points for each number)

1. know, no
2. threw, through
3. do, dew
4. wore, war
5. hear, here
6. sum, some
7. piece, peace
8. There, their
9. rays, raise
10. heard, herd

D. (Bold letters indicate circled answers.)

1. cr **y** ing
2. twent **y**
3.
4. donke **y**
5. sk **y**
6.
7. tr **y**
8. gentl **y**
9. fr **y**
10.
11. cit **y**
12.
13. happ **y**
14. bu **y**
15. m **y**
16. read **y**
17.
18. fl **y** ing
19. angr **y**
20. an **y** thing
21. sh **y**
22. wh **y**
23. ferr **y**
24.

***y* says /ī/**

crying	fry	flying
sky	buy	shy
try	my	why

(One point for each circle and one for each written word)

***y* says /ē/**

twenty	city	angry
donkey	happy	anything
gently	ready	ferry

Gradebook: 98 points

LESSON 20
The Quarrel Is Settled

I. Preparing to Read

Pointer Questions

1. Why was Amasa supposed to gather the men of Judah together?
2. Who kept the city of Abel from being destroyed?

II. Reader

Discussion

"Who was David's new captain? What job did David give Amasa to do? How did he fail?

"What harm might Sheba have been doing? [He could have been gaining the support of the people of Israel to work against David.] Whom did David send after Sheba? Who else went without being sent? Where did they meet Amasa? What had Amasa lost on the way? What did Joab do with it?

"Why do you think Joab would want to kill Amasa? [He may have resented the fact that Amasa replaced him as captain.] Was Amasa a good captain? [He took more than three days to gather the people. He did not notice when he lost the sword, nor that Joab had it in his hand.]

"Where was Sheba? What did Joab and the other men do when they got there? Who got them to stop beating on the wall? How did she do it?

"What did Joab do after Sheba was dead? What was given to Joab again at Jerusalem? [position of captain]"

III. Workbook

ANSWER KEY

A.
1. Sheba
2. Amasa
3. David
4. David
5. David
6. Joab
7. Amasa
8. Amasa
9. Joab
10. Joab
11. Joab
12. A woman
13. A woman
14. A woman
15. A woman

B.

2	8	12	13	19
4	7	9	15	20
1	6	11	16	17
3	5	10	14	18

C.
1. Joab could not be captain because he had *killed Absalom.*
2. He wanted to go to *battle against Sheba.*
3. a. He *did not come back* as soon as he was told to.
   b. He *did not notice* when he dropped his sword.
4. They wanted to get *Sheba,* who was in the city.
5. A *wise woman talked* to Joab and had Sheba killed.

D.
1. urged
2. understood
3. pretend
4. clothes
5. put out
6. pay back
7. driven out
8. think out
9. did as he said

10. spot
11. dried
12. cut
13. top
14. hate
15. cubs
16. disorder

LESSON 21
Israel Makes Things Right

I. Preparing to Read

Pointer Questions

1. Why was it wrong to kill the Gibeonites?
2. What did Joab do that he did not want to do?

II. Reader

Test comprehension with this oral quiz. Have the children write brief answers to your questions.

1. For how many years was there a famine in Israel? (three)
2. Who told David why the famine came? (God)
3. Who killed some Gibeonites? (Saul)
4. How many sons of Saul did David give to the Gibeonites? (seven)
5. Did David give Mephibosheth to the Gibeonites? (no)
6. Where did the Gibeonites hang the sons of Saul? (on a hill)
7. Did the Gibeonites bury the sons of Saul? (no)
8. With what did the son of a giant intend to kill David? (a new spear)
9. Who saved David from being killed? (Joab's brother)
10. Why did David's servants not want him to go to battle? (He was getting older.)
11. How many fingers were on each hand of the giant from Gath? (six)
12. How many toes were on each foot of the giant from Gath? (six)
13. Who killed that giant? (David's nephew)
14. How many sons of the giant did Israel kill altogether? (four)
15. Who wanted to have all the people counted? (David)
16. Who did not think they should be counted? (Joab)
17. About how long did it take to number the people? (ten months)
18. Did they count all the people? (no)
19. Were there 1½ thousand or 1½ million men who could handle a spear and go to war? (million)
20. Did Joab go back to Jerusalem after counting the people? (yes)

Extra Activity

You may want to assign some students to research some of the Bible stories referred to in this lesson and report on these questions.

1. Why was it wrong to kill the Gibeonites? (Joshua 9:3–15)
2. What agreement had David made with Jonathan? (1 Samuel 20:11–17)

III. Workbook

ANSWER KEY

A.
1. Saul and his men had *killed the Gibeonites.*
2. Israel had *promised they would not* destroy them.
3. David had made an *agreement with Jonathan.*
4. They *did not want David to be killed.*
5. *The Lord* helped them.
6. He thought *God would not be pleased.*
7. *David insisted* that they should be numbered.

B.
1. c
2. a
3. b
4. b
5. a
6. b
7. b
8. a

C.
1. slow
2. kings
3. parents
4. tall
5. wrong
6. mouths
7. green
8. dangerous
9. busy
10. babies
11. drink
12. warm
13. seen
14. happiness
15. small
16. opened
17. short

D.
1. slain
faint
strain
raise
2. again
against
said
3. certain
Captain

LESSON 22
God Punishes Israel

I. Preparing to Read

Pointer Questions

1. What were the choices of punishment for David?
2. What did David see over Jerusalem?

II. Reader

Discussion

"For what was God going to send a punishment? What three punishments could David choose from? Which one did he choose? Why did he choose that one?

"How many people died in those three days? From what did they die? [Wherever God's angel stretched out his sword, a pestilence came upon the people and they died.] Where was the angel when God told him to destroy no more?

"What sheep was David talking about? [He was comparing his people to sheep that depend on their leader for care and safety. If danger or suffering comes to the sheep, it is not the fault of the sheep, but the shepherd's responsibility. These innocent people were dying because of David's sin.]

"Who told David to set up an altar? Where was it to be?

"What did Ornan and his sons do when the angel appeared? Why? What did Ornan want to do when David said he wanted to buy the threshing floor? Why did David insist on paying for the things? How much did he pay? What did he do with the things he bought?"

III. Workbook

You might want to discuss some of the items in part D. Number 10 is a question of personal preference rather than sound judgment.

ANSWER KEY

A. I. A. of famine
- B. of fleeing from enemies
- C. of pestilence

II. A. into the hand of God.
- B. a pestilence.
- C. people died.
- D. over Jerusalem to destroy it.

III. A. to hold back his hand.
- B. an altar
- C. the plague.

IV. A. sackcloth.
- B. who had sinned.
- C. on him and his house.
- D. Ornan's threshing floor.
- E. an altar.
- F. burnt offerings and peace offerings.

B. 1. Uriah
2. seventy-thousand people
3. David
4. yes

C. 1. to ~~had~~ number
2. prophet ~~to~~ Gad
3. ~~for~~
4. ~~good~~
5. ~~long~~
6. days ~~when~~ of
7. rather ~~would~~ fall
8. ~~back~~ (either one)
9. ~~after~~
10. ~~then~~
11. ~~to~~
12. ~~look~~
13. ~~more~~
14. ~~from~~
15. ~~on~~

D. 1. a
2. a
3. b
4. b
5. b
6. a
7. b
8. a
9. b
10. (Individual answers)

E. 1.
2. build
3.
4
5.
6. guide
7. guilt
8. plague
9. buy
10. built
11.
12. guess

vowel

LESSON 23
David Plans a House for God

I. Preparing to Read

Pointer Questions

1. Who would build the house for God?
2. What was used for God's house before this time?

II. Reader

Discussion

"Why could David not build God's house?

"Whose son was Solomon? [David's. God also said, "He shall be My son." God calls those who obey Him His children.]

"What had David prepared for God's house? Who else did he tell to take part in the work of building?

"Why was a tent best for God's house in the days of Moses? Where were they going? Why was it unsuitable to build a temple in Canaan before this time? How could the people be sure they would not have wars now to keep them from building?

"Where was the temple to be built?"

III. Workbook

Help the children to understand the outline structure under part III. A and B are divided into numbered subpoints.

ANSWER KEY

A.

I. A. young and tender
   B. exceeding magnificent

II. A. build the house
   B. with the work
   C. wisdom and understanding. (You may also accept *rest, peace and quietness.*)
   D. strong and of good courage

III. A. 1. Gold
      2. Silver
      3. Brass
      4. Iron
      5. Timber
      6. Stone
   B. of workmen.
      1. kinds of work.
      2. to do their work well.

IV. A. Solomon
   B. their heart and soul to find out what God wanted them to do
   C. and build the house

V. A. traveling
   B. many wars
   C. many wars.

VI. A. peace

B.

1. b
2. a
3. b
4. a
5. b
6. b
7. b
8. a
9. a
10. a
11. a

C. (Accept words with similar meaning.)

1. bad
2. short

3. closed
4. clean
5. death
6. clear
7. well
8 hot
9. wide
10. dry
11. forget

D. 1. round
house
about
out
2. should
would
could
3. youth
you
4. courage
discourage
5. soul

LESSON 24
Adonijah Wants to be King

I. Preparing to Read

Pointer Questions

1. Who agreed to help Adonijah become king?
2. How did Adonijah prepare for the celebration?

II. Reader

Discussion

"Why did Israel need another king? Who did God plan should be the next king? Who tried to take the kingdom for himself? Which of David's sons was he? What kind of person was he?

"Whom did Adonijah get to help him in his plans? Why did Nathan and Zadok not help him? What did Adonijah do?

"Who was the only son of David who was not called to the celebration? Why do you think he was excluded? [Perhaps Adonijah knew of David's intention to have Solomon reign.]

"Why do you think Nathan planned that Bath-sheba and he should both report Adonijah's doings to David? [He may have done that to make sure David realized how serious the matter was.] How serious was it? [Solomon and his mother would be killed if Adonijah was let go.]

"What did David promise to do about it?

"What did Bath-sheba say after David made his promise? Old and feeble as David was, did Bath-sheba think he would not die? Why would she say that he should live forever? ['Live forever' was a standard greeting of great respect and honor. Perhaps it could be taken as a wish that the person could live forever.]"

III. Workbook

ANSWER KEY

A.
1. Adonijah
2. Bath-sheba
3. Solomon
4. Adonijah
5. Abiathar
6. Nathan
7. Zadok
8. David
9. Bath-sheba
10. Nathan
11. Bath-sheba
12. Joab
13. Adonijah, Abiathar, Joab, captains, the king's sons

B.

1. himself	11. Nathan
2. kingdom	12. older
3. should	13. oxen
4. sheep	14. priest
5. promise	15. Bath-sheba
6. Solomon	16. bedroom
7. throne	17. respect
8. cattle	18. brothers
9. together	19. ground
10. prophet	20. king

C.

1. old	5. He
2. own	6. except
3. what	7. many
4. talking	8. killed

D.
1. respectful
2. spoiled
3. envious
4. thoughtful
5. careless
6. godly
7. honest

E.
1. older, oldest
2. harder, hardest
3. warmer, warmest
4. faster, fastest
5. younger, youngest
6. greater, greatest
7. stronger, strongest
8. deeper, deepest
9. kinder, kindest
10. shorter, shortest

LESSON 25
"God Save King Solomon!"

I. Preparing to Read

Pointer Questions

1. Where was Solomon anointed king?
2. How did Adonijah and his followers respond to the news of Solomon's anointing?

II. Reader

Discussion

"Repeat the directions David gave for having Solomon anointed king.

"What kind of blessing were David's servants saying for Solomon?

"What sounds did Adonijah and his followers hear at the end of their feast? [trumpet, shouting, piping on pipes] Who told them what the noise meant? Why do you suppose everyone was so fearful right away? [They must have been aware that they were opposing the plan of God and King David.]

"What did Adonijah do? Why?

"What did Solomon say about killing Adonijah?

"What was David's last message to Solomon?

"How old was David when he died? How long had he been king? Where was he buried?"

III. Workbook

ANSWER KEY

A.

1	9
5	7
4	8
3	6
2	10

B.
1. They were to blow the trumpet *after Solomon was anointed.*
2. Solomon rode King *David's mule.*
3. Zadok took a horn of oil from the *tabernacle.*
4. The *trumpet,* the *shouting,* the *piping* on pipes, and crowds of people walking could be heard among the people who followed Solomon.

C.

Across	*Down*
1. Gihon	2. oil
3. man	4. name
7. Solomon	5. guests
9. horn	6. prophet
10. years	7. seventy
12. valiant	8. Nathan
14. throne	11. amen
15. Jonathan	13. anoint
17. altar	16. hairs
19. city	18. ruler
21. trumpet	20. mule
22. shall	

D.

1. b	12. a
2. a	13. c
3. b	14. a
4. a	15. b
5. a	16. a
6. b	17. c
7. c	18. b
8. b	19. a
9. a	20. c
10. b	21. b
11. c	

E.
1. wider, widest
2. later, latest
3. wiser, wisest
4. cuter, cutest
5. nicer, nicest
6. finer, finest
7. larger, largest
8. stranger, strangest

(Two points for each number)

Gradebook: 74 points

LESSON 26
Solomon Prepares for a Peaceable Reign

I. Preparing to Read

Pointer Questions

1. Who were the unworthy men in Solomon's kingdom?
2. How long was it until Solomon had Shimei killed?

II. Reader

Discussion

"What did Solomon do first in his kingdom?
"Why was Adonijah punished?
"Why was Abiathar punished? How was he punished?
"Why was Joab punished?
"Why was Shimei punished? How was he punished?
"How would these punishments help other people in Solomon's kingdom?

III. Workbook

ANSWER KEY

A. 1. d
2. b
3. a
4. c

B. death, slain, killed

C. I. A. Adonijah
B. Abiathar
C. Joab
D. Shimei

II. A. risen up against David (*or* not shown himself worthy.)
B. helped Adonijah.
C. killed two men more righteous than he.
D. cursed David (or left Jerusalem.)

III. A. put to death
B. not allowed to be priest.
C. killed
D. made to stay in Jerusalem (*or* killed).

IV. A. be enemies to Solomon.
B. his kingdom with peace.

D. 1. *Zadok* was made priest.
2. *Benaiah* was made captain.
3. Shimei *went after his servants* that ran away.

E. 1. overtake
2. overcome
3. overflow
4. overcoat
5. overload
6. oversight
7. overhead
8. understand
9. underbrush
10. underground
11. underneath
12. undertake
13. undertone
14. underweight
15. homemade
16. homeland
17. homeless
18. homesick
19. homespun
20. homework
21. homeward

22. outstretched
23. outstanding
24. outlook
25. outgrow
26. outlying
27. outside
28. outline

LESSON 27
God Gives Solomon Great Wisdom

I. Preparing to Read

Pointer Questions

1. For what did Solomon ask God?
2. What did God give that he had not asked?

II. Reader

Discussion

"What was Solomon doing at Gibeon? When did God tell Solomon to ask for anything he wanted? Why did Solomon choose what he did?

"Why did God also give Solomon riches and honor? That is an example of the blessing of unselfishness. Solomon did not ask for something to make him great, and he was blessed with things he did not expect.

"What test of his wisdom soon came? How did Solomon discover who was the child's real mother?

"How well was Solomon known for his wisdom? How many wise sayings did he speak? How many songs did he sing?

"How many horses and chariots did Solomon have? How was Israel blessed in his days?"

III. Workbook

ANSWER KEY

A.
1. b
2. c
3. a
4. c
5. b, c
6. b, d, f
7. a
8. a

B.
1. *Two women* came to Solomon.
2. They both wanted *the same child.*
3. Solomon said it should be *divided* with a sword.
4. She *did not want the child to be killed,* because she loved him.
5. He knew the *one who loved the child* was the mother.

C.
1. slow
2. friends
3. thirsty
4. pit
5. praise
6. Rejoice
7. rich
8. Wine
9. life
10. foolish
11. loveth
12. trusteth
13. soft
14. Lord

15. just
16. fire
17. hate
18. son
19. vinegar
20. fruit

D.
1. b
2. b
3. b
4. a
5. b
6. a
7. a
8. a
9. b
10. b

E.
1. 4
2. 5
3. 3
4. 2
5. 7
6. 3
7. 5
8. 6
9. 1
10. 4
11. 5
12. 7
13. 6
14. 3
15. 4
16. 2
17. 2
18. 3
19. 6
20. 1
21. 4

LESSON 28
Solomon Builds the Temple

I. Preparing to Read

Pointer Questions

1. Whom did Solomon ask for help in making the temple?
2. Why was there no noise when the temple was built?

II. Reader

Test comprehension with this oral quiz. Have the children write an answer from the choice given in each question. (Answers in italics)

1. Was Tyre along the *Great Sea* or the Jordan River?
2. Was Hiram the king of Lebanon or *Tyre*?
3. Was Lebanon a *mountain* or a city?
4. Did Solomon want Hiram to send him gold or *trees*?
5. Did Solomon's request make Hiram *happy* or angry?
6. Did they send the trees on the *sea* or on the river?
7. Did Solomon get the trees at Jericho or *Joppa*?
8. Did Solomon pay Hiram with money or *food*?
9. Did the men work in the mountains in groups of *ten thousand* or thirty thousand?
10. Were the workers at home for one month or *two months* at a time?
11. Were more men used to *cut stones* or to carry stones?
12. Had Solomon appointed two thousand or *three thousand* rulers over the workers?
13. Did it take four or *seven* years to build the temple?
14. Inside the finished temple, could one see wood or *gold* on the walls, ceiling, and floor?
15. Was the *ark* or the tabernacle put into the temple?
16. Was a sea made for the *priests to wash in* or for the oxen to drink from?

17. Was the sea made of *metal* or wood?
18. Did the sea hold *twenty* or thirty thousand gallons of water?
19. Was the temple decorated with paintings or *carvings*?
20. Was the temple on *Mount Moriah* or Mount Olivet?

III. Workbook

You may want to clarify the heading *Minerals* in part C as meaning "rocks and metals."

Discuss the map in part D. Can the children find the Great Sea? Explain that *Mediterranean Sea* is its modern name. Explain the compound words used as directions in numbers 7 and 8. Northwest is somewhere between north and west. Northeast is between north and east, and so forth.

ANSWER KEY

A.
1. 30,000
2. 10,000; 1; 2
3. 80,000; 70,000
4. 3,000

B.

1.	no	9.	yes
2.	yes	10.	no
3.	yes	11.	no
4.	no	12.	no
5.	yes	13.	no
6.	no	14.	yes
7.	yes	15.	yes
8.	no	16.	no

C.
1. Joppa
   Jerusalem
   Bethlehem
   Hebron
2. Galilee
   Canaan
   Egypt
   Syria
3. Barzillai
   Mephibosheth
   Nathan
   Ittai
4. Shimei
   Hanun
   Absalom
   Adonijah
5. algum
   cedar
   oak
   fir
6. brass
   iron
   gold
   silver
7. Sinai
   Olivet
   Gilboa
   Lebanon
8. unsuitable
   gracious
   magnificent
   handsome

D.
1. (1 beside *Lebanon Mountains*)
2. (2 beside *Tyre*)
3. (3 beside *Mediterranean Sea*)
4. (4 beside *Joppa*)
5. (5 beside *Jerusalem*)
6. (*NORTH, SOUTH, EAST, and WEST* printed at the correct places)
7. southwest
8. southeast
9. 30 miles

E.

1. 2	9. 1	17. 6
2. 6	10. 3	18. 1
3. 4	11. 2	19. 5
4. 1	12. 6	20. 1
5. 2	13. 3	21. 3
6. 5	14. 2	22. 1, 5
7. 3	15. 6	23. 1, 4
8. 3	16. 1	24. 1, 4

LESSON 29
Solomon's Glorious Reign

I. Preparing to Read

Pointer Questions

1. What special signs did God show when the temple was dedicated?
2. Why did the Queen of Sheba come to Solomon?

II. Reader

Discussion

"What things did the people do at the temple dedication?

"What did God promise when He came to Solomon in the night?

"How long did it take Solomon to build his own house? What else did he build?

"What did the Queen of Sheba bring with her?

"Do you know any questions that would be very hard to answer?

"What did the Queen of Sheba see at Solomon's house that impressed her?

"How did Solomon get his great riches?"

III. Workbook

ANSWER KEY

A.

1. the ark of God
2. a cloud / the glory of God
3. before the altar
4. blessed the people
5. fire
6. burned the offering
7. seven days
8. seven days
9. fourteen
10. a solemn meeting
11. too many to count
12. thirteen

B.

1. b	4. c
2. b	5. c
3. a	6. a

C.
1. magnificent
   worship
   large
   costly
   holy
2. wise
   kind
   godly
   rich
3. happy
   willing
   capable
   wise
8. willing
9. complaining
10. large
11. rich
12. thoughtless
13. wise
14. few
15. magnificent
16. ugly
17. noisy
18. godly
19. worship
20. covetous

D.
1. lazy
2. capable
3. costly
4. happy
5. holy
6. old
7. kind

E.

1. 3	8. 1	15. 2
2. 3	9. 3	16. 4
3. 2	10. 2	17. 1
4. 1	11. 4	18. 3
5. 1	12. 1	19. 4
6. 1	13. 3	20. 4
7. 2	14. 1	21. 2

LESSON 30
A Very Sad End

I. Preparing to Read

Pointer Questions

1. What commandment did Solomon break?
2. What did the twelve pieces of Jeroboam's garment represent?

II. Reader

Discussion

"How many years did the children of Israel travel in the wilderness? How many years did they live in Canaan before the wars were all over?

"What were some of Israel's blessings in Solomon's time?

"What did Solomon do that was wrong? What was God going to do because of Solomon's sin? When would He do it?

"Why did Solomon make Jeroboam a ruler?

"Who tore Jeroboam's new garment? How many pieces did he make? What did the pieces represent? How many tribes would Jeroboam rule? How many tribes would Solomon's son rule? Do ten and one make twelve?

Solomon's son would rule the large tribe of Judah. The small tribe of Benjamin would support him also, but the whole kingdom was called Judah. So the name *Judah* actually represented two pieces of the garment.

"How did Solomon like the idea of Jeroboam being king? How did Jeroboam avoid being killed by Solomon?

"Which of Solomon's sons became king when Solomon died? Where was Solomon buried? What city is the city of David?"

III. Workbook

You may want to assign names in part C to make sure the list is covered. For a large class, you might assign each student part of his ten names and let him select his choice for the rest.

ANSWER KEY

A.
1. S
2.
3.
4. S
5. S
6. S
7.
8. S
9.
10. S
11.
12.

9. Solomon
10. Ahijah
11. Rehoboam
12. Solomon
13. David
14. Rehoboam

B.
1. Solomon
2. God or Moses
3. Solomon
4. His wives
5. David's
6. Solomon's son
7. Jeroboam
8. Jeroboam

C. (Individual sentences)

D.
1. 4
2. 1
3. 4
4. 3
5. 4
6. 3
7. 2
8. 3
9. 4
10. 2
11. 1
12. 4
13. 1
14. 4
15. 4
16. 2
17. 1
18. 2
19. 3
20. 2
21. 4

TEST

ANSWER KEY

A.

1. no
2. no
3. no
4. no
5. no
6. no
7. yes
8. yes
9. no
10. no
11. no
12. yes
13. yes
14. yes
15. no

B.

1. d
2. c
3. e
4. a
5. b
6. j
7. i
8. h
9. g
10. f
11. l
12. o
13. m
14. k
15. n
16. p
17. r
18. q
19. t
20. s

C.

1. Solomon asked for *wisdom.*
2. David was a *man of war.*
3. There was *no noise* when the temple was built.
4. Uzzah died because he *touched the ark.*

Gradebook: 39 points

Unit Two

Stories of the Kings—Rehoboam to Jeroboam

UNIT 2
General Plan

I. Preparing to Read

Evaluate the routine procedure for study of the new words. Is it effective? Motivate the children to be well prepared by asking them to read the list of new words and give definitions by memory at the beginning of oral reading class.

Suggested pointer questions are provided for direction in silent reading and oral discussion.

II. Reader

Renew efforts to achieve good quality in oral reading. (See procedure for grading oral reading in Lesson 16 of Unit 1.)

Suggested questions are given for class discussion that involve deeper thinking than just memory of the story details. Do not omit the detail questions. Jot some in the margin of your reader as you prepare for class, or underline pertinent details from which to frame questions. The thought questions suggested in the manual may be jotted in the margin of your reader as well for convenience.

III. Workbook

Remove and file the unit tests before distributing the workbooks.

Inside the front and back covers of the workbook is a time line chart for the reigns of the kings of Judah and Israel. Instructions are given in the workbook lessons and information is provided to fill in the charts as you proceed through the unit.

The completed chart for Unit 2 is shown on pages 64 and 65 with lesson numbers indicating where the information is found.

Unit 2 Lessons

Lesson **Page**

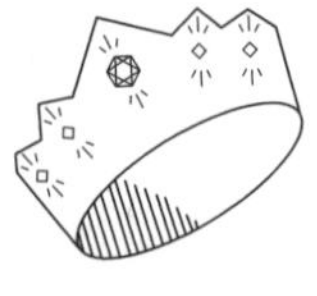

KINGS

Saul
David
Solomon

JUDAH		ISRAEL
1. Rehoboam (1) a. Solomon's son (1) b. reigned 17 years (2)	930 B.C.	1. Jeroboam (1) a. Nebat's son (1) b. Solomon's servant (1) c. caused Israel to sin (2) d. reigned 22 years (6)
	920 B.C.	
2. Abijah (6) a. Rehoboam's son (6) b. reigned 3 years (6)		
3. Asa (6) a. Abijah's son (6) b. heart perfect before God (7) c. reigned 41 years (7)	910 B.C.	2. Nadab (6) a. Jeroboam's son—2 years (6) 3. Baasha (6) a. from another tribe (6) b. killed Nadab (7) c. reigned about 23 years (7)
	900 B.C.	

JUDAH	890 B.C.	ISRAEL
		4. Elah, Baasha's son (7) a. reigned parts of 2 years (7)
		5. Zimri—reigned 7 days (7)
	880 B.C.	6. Omri (7) a. commander of Elah's armies (7) b. reigned about 17 years (7)
4. Jehoshaphat (7) a. Asa's son (7) b. reigned 25 years (20)	870 B.C	7. Ahab (7) a. Omri's son (7) b. wicked wife Jezebel (7) c. reigned 22 years (18)
	860 B.C	
		8. Ahaziah (18) a. Ahab's son—2 years (18)
	850 B.C.	9. Jehoram (20) a. Ahaziah's brother (20)

LESSON 1
The Kingdom Divides

I. Preparing to Read

Pointer Questions

1. Who was Rehoboam's father?
2. Why did the people not want Rehoboam to be their king?

II. Reader

"From what mistakes of Solomon's could the older men have learned? [many wives, idol worship, overworking his people]

"Why is it better to follow the advice of older men than younger men? Did you ever look down from a mountain and see many houses, fields, and roads? Down in the valley you could have a good view of your house and perhaps your neighbors' houses and the road that runs by your house. But from the mountain you can have a much broader view.

"We can compare that to the way we see things in life. Young men have not gone very far in their journey of life. They may see many things that are interesting and good, but there are many things they have not seen yet. A godly young man may give some advice that is good, but he has many things to learn yet.

"Older men are like people who have climbed higher on the mountain. They have seen more things and have a broader view of life. They can see where a road leads that someone in the valley can see for just a short distance. Because they are older, they understand more things and can give better advice. It is wise to follow the counsel of godly old men.

"What did Rehoboam do to make the people submit to him? [He sent out a tax officer and later prepared for war.] How did the people show that they would not submit? [They stoned the officer.]

III. Workbook

A timesaver for slow students would be to have them list the numbers instead of writing out the sentences for answers to part A.

ANSWER KEY

A. *The Table of Contents*

(2) It gives the titles of the stories in the reader.

(3) It is at the beginning of the reader.

(7) It tells you on which pages to find the stories in the reader.

(8) It gives the order in which the stories come in the reader.

(10) It helps you to find a story quickly.

The Glossary

(1) It gives a list of the new words in the reader.

(4) It is at the back of the reader.

(5) It tells you how to pronounce words.

(6) It is in alphabetical order.

(9) It tells the meanings of words.

B. 1. yes, 4
2. yes, 3
3. yes, 3
4. yes, 5
5. yes, 8
6. yes, 10

C. 1. yes
2. no
3. no
4. no

D. 1. (*NORTH* and *SOUTH* printed in provided boxes)
2. Israel
3. Judah
4. Dan
5. Bethel
6. (Shechem circled)
7. (*Jerusalem* beside the star in Judah)
8. (*Samaria* beside the star in Israel)
9. (a line to Shechem from edge of map near arrow indicating Egypt)
10. (Jordan River, Dead Sea, and Mediterranean Sea labeled)

E. 1. A capital city is the city *where the king lives* and rules.
2. The kingdom of *Israel* was larger.
3. Shemaiah told him that the *Lord said he should not.*

F. 1.
2.
3.
4. advice
5.
6.
7. decided
8. cities
9.
10. officers
11.
12. force
13.
14. city
15. mercy
16.
17. incense
18. icy
19.
20. sacrifice
21. merciful

(Information to be on the chart in the front of the workbook)

Judah:
1. Rehoboam
   a. Solomon's son

Israel:
1. Jeroboam
   a. Nebat's son
   b. Solomon's servant

LESSON 2
Jeroboam Causes Israel to Sin

I. Preparing to Read

Pointer Questions

1. What did Jeroboam say the golden calves had done?
2. What changes did Jeroboam make in the people's worship?
3. What did the people do who still wanted to serve the Lord?

II. Reader

"How did Jeroboam get the kingdom? [God chose him.] Why did he think he might lose it? [He thought the people would return to Rehoboam because of their worship.] What did he do to prevent that? [He turned the people away from God.]

"Why could Judah not overcome the army from Egypt? [They had turned away from God.] What kept them from being destroyed completely? [They humbled themselves.]"

III. Workbook

ANSWER KEY

A.

1. c	7. a
2. b	8. c
3. a	9. c
4. c	10. a
5. b	11. a
6. b	12. c

B.
1. glossary
2. table of contents
3. table of contents
4. glossary
5. table of contents
6. table of contents
7. glossary
8. glossary
9. glossary
10. glossary

C.
I. (Accept any two.)
Leave him
Join themselves to Rehoboam
Kill him

II. A. idols
B. 1. Bethel
2. Dan
C. anyone
D. in the eighth month

III. A. He sinned.
B. He caused Israel to sin.

D.
1. humble
2. humbled
3. humbly
4. righteous, right
5. righteousness

E.

1.	8.
2. Egypt	9.
3.	10. huge
4.	11.
5.	12.
6.	13. strange
7. charge	14.

15.
16.
17. giant
18. danger
19.
20. angel
21. Egyptian

get, give

(Information to be on the chart in the front of the workbook)

Judah:

1. b. reigned 17 years

Israel:

1. c. caused Israel to sin

LESSON 3
A Man of God Comes to Bethel

I. Preparing to Read

Pointer Questions

1. What miracles happened in this story?
2. What special instructions were given to the man of God?

II. Reader

"Why do you suppose the old prophet had such a great interest in talking to the man of God? [Perhaps he was seeking the truth. Perhaps he wanted to discuss memories of godliness and blessings that were no longer found in Israel. As a prophet he may have had some things in common with the man of God.]"

III. Workbook

In part B have the children locate the word *or* in sample questions and identify the answer choices—one on either side of the *or.*

Consider a few samples in part C with the class.

ANSWER KEY

A.
1. Rehoboam
2. Rehoboam
3. Jeroboam
4. Rehoboam
5. Rehoboam
6. Jeroboam
7. Jeroboam
8. Rehoboam
9. Rehoboam
10. Jeroboam
11. Rehoboam
12. Rehoboam
13. Jeroboam
14. Jeroboam
15. Rehoboam
16. Rehoboam
17. Rehoboam
18. Jeroboam
19. Jeroboam
20. Jeroboam

B. (Accept variation in the amount of words underlined. Answers given here are key words which must be included in the answer.)

2. incense
3. Judah
4. altar
5. bones
6. born later
7. king
8. sign
9. wither
10. draw his hand back
11. pray
12. made well
13. king invite the man of God
14. reward
15. not
16. old
17. donkey

C.
1. who
2. when
3. where
4. why
5. who
6. why
7. where
8. why
9. when
10. who
11. where

D. restored, refresh, reward, return

1. repair
2. remember
3. return
4. reflection
5. refresh
6. replace
7. rebuild
8. repay
9. restore
10. renew
11. reread
12. recount
13. respell
14. retell
15. refill
16. reprint
17. reset
18. retake

LESSON 4
The Disobedient Prophet

I. Preparing to Read

Pointer Questions

1. How did the old prophet persuade the man of God to go back with him?
2. What was unusual about the lion's behavior?

II. Reader

"Do you think the old prophet wanted to get the man of God into trouble? Did he plan to say what he did at the table? [He probably had no evil intent in having the man come back to talk, and lied because he was so determined to have him come. At the table he delivered the message that came to him then from the Lord.]"

III. Workbook

Make sure the children know how to count paragraphs in the reader when there are single-line paragraphs.

ANSWER KEY

A.
1. no
2. no
3. no
4. yes
5. no
6. yes
7. yes
8. no
9. no
10. no
11. no
12. no
13. yes
14. no
15. yes
16. yes
17. yes
18. no
19. yes
20. yes
21. yes
22. yes

B.
1. 10—saddle the donkey, (or) 12—bury him with the man of God
2. 7—a lion
3. 5—an angel
4. 5—what the old prophet said
5. 6—when they were sitting at the table
6. 12—beside the man of God
7. 7—when they had finished eating
8. 9—he was disobedient
9. 8—some men
10. 11—back to the city
11. 11—"Alas, my brother!"

C.
1. c, left
2. a, left
3. b, left
4. b, hard
5. a, hard
6. c, hard

7. a, scorpions
8. b, Scorpions
9. b, rough
10. a, rough
11. c, rough
12. b, ruler
13. a, ruler
14. b, house
15. a, house
16. a, capital
17. b, capital
18. b, pounds
19. a, pounds
20. b, back
21. c, back
22. a, back
23. a, table
24. b, table

D. 1. ou
2. ou
3. oo
4. $\overline{\text{oo}}$
5. ou
6. ou
7. ô
8. ô
9. oo
10. ô
11. $\overline{\text{oo}}$
12. oo

LESSON 5
Sad News

I. Preparing to Read

Pointer Questions

1. Why did Jeroboam think Ahijah could tell him if his son would live?
2. How did Ahijah know it was Jeroboam's wife who came?

II. Reader

"Why would Abijah be the only one buried? What would happen to the rest of Jeroboam's family?

"What did the Lord mean when He said a king of Israel would destroy the house of Jeroboam? [All his family members would be destroyed, not necessarily the building in which he lived.]"

III. Workbook

Do a few numbers in part B together with the class.

ANSWER KEY

A. 1. Abijah
2. Ahijah
3. Shiloh
4. disguise
5. ten, cakes, honey
6. old, see
7. The Lord, pretend
8. prince
9. David
10. evil
11. provoke
12. dogs, birds
13. king
14. fathers, scatter

B. 1. then
2. now
3. both
4. both
5. then
6. then
7. now
8. both
9. both
10. now
11. both
12. both
13. both
14. both

C.
1. He *heard the sound of her feet* when Jeroboam's wife came.
2. Ahijah had *told him he would be king,* and that came to pass.
3. He *kept God's commandments.*
4. He did *more evil than anyone before* him.
5. He *made other gods.*

D.
1. a
2. c
3. a
4. c
5. b
6. b
7. b
8. c
9. c
10. c

Gradebook: 48 points

LESSON 6
Israel Disobeys

I. Preparing to Read

Pointer Questions

1. Who started the battle?
2 Who won the battle?

II. Reader

"How did Abijah describe Rehoboam at the time the kingdom divided? Do you think Rehoboam was tenderhearted?

"Why did Abijah reason that God was on Judah's side? [The people of Judah kept the sacrifices and laws of God.]

"How many children did Abijah have? [22 + 16 = 38]"

III. Workbook

ANSWER KEY

A.
1. Abijah
2. Josiah
3. A man of God
4. Ahijah
5. Jeroboam
6. An old prophet
7. Abijah
8. Nadab
9. Baasha
10. Rehoboam

B.
1. God
2. Rehoboam
3. yes
4. every morning and evening
5. no
6. yes
7. yes
8. yes
9. behind them and in front of them
10. Judah called upon God
11. three years
12. Asa
13. two years after Asa became king
14. yes
15. no
16. no

C.

4	8	11	19
3	7	13	18
5	10	12	17
1	6	15	20
2	9	14	16

D.
1. cl ***ou*** d
2. t ***ow*** n
3. sh ***ou*** t
4. h ***ou*** se
5. h ***ow***
6. fr ***ow*** n
7. pl ***ow***
8. m ***ou*** th
9. ***ou*** r
10. gr ***ow*** l
11. n ***ow***
12. ar ***ou*** nd
13. ***ow*** l
14. cr ***ow*** n
15. s ***ou*** th
16. th ***ou*** sand
17. h ***ow*** l
18. c ***ow***

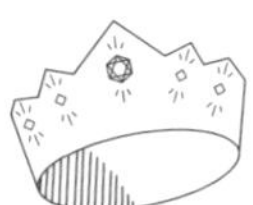

(Information to be on the kings chart)

Judah:

2. Abijah
   a. Rehoboam's son
   b. reigned 3 years
3. Asa
   a. Abijah's son

Israel:

1. d. reigned 22 years
2. Nadab
   a. Jeroboam's son—2 years
3. Baasha
   a. from another tribe

LESSON 7
Good King Asa

I. Preparing to Read

Pointer Questions

1. What things did Asa do to bring Judah back to God?
2. On what two occasions did Asa fail to ask God for help?

II. Reader

"Why did some of the people of Israel come over to Judah?

"What did the prophet mean when he said, 'The eyes of the Lord run to and fro throughout the whole earth to show Himself strong in behalf of those whose hearts are perfect toward Him'? [God looks all around in the earth to find people with hearts that are right toward Him. Then He helps them with His strength.]"

III. Workbook

ANSWER KEY

A.

1. h	7. e	13. k
2. g	8. f	14. p
3. a	9. j	15. l
4. c	10. i	16. m
5. d	11. o	
6. b	12. n	

B.
1. ~~Israel~~, Judah
2. ~~thousand~~, million
3. ~~thought~~, knew
4. ~~lose~~, overcome
5. ~~most~~, some
6. ~~five~~, seven

7. ~~trust~~, serve
8. ~~men~~, people
9. ~~Before~~, After
10. ~~priest~~, king
11. ~~hear~~, see
12. ~~remained~~, reminded
13. ~~knees~~, feet

C. (Possible sentences)

He broke the idols his father had made.

He took away the altars of the strange gods.

He commanded the people to come back to God and obey Him.

He did not let his mother be queen, because of the idol she made.

He trusted God when an enemy came with a million people.

He destroyed idols in Judah and Benjamin.

He set up the altar of the Lord.

D. (Possible sentences)

He called upon a heathen king for help.

He became angry with the prophet and put him into prison.

He did not go to the Lord for help when he got sick.

E.

1. j ***oy***
2. t ***oy***
3. j ***oi*** n
4. t ***oi*** l
5. ***oi*** l
6. s ***oy***
7. sp ***oi*** l
8. m ***oi*** st
9. R ***oy***
10. s ***oi*** l
11. destr ***oy***
12. c ***oy***
13. c ***oi*** l
14. p ***oi*** nt
15. h ***oi*** st
16. c ***oi*** n
17. enj ***oy***
18. empl ***oy***
19. rej ***oi*** ce
20. p ***oi*** son

(Information to be on the kings chart)

Judah:

3. b. heart perfect before God
   c. reigned 41 years
4. Jehoshaphat (back cover)
   a. Asa's son

Israel:

3. b. killed Nadab
   c. reigned about 23 years
4. Elah, Baasha's son (back cover)
   a. reigned parts of 2 years
5. Zimri—reigned 7 days
6. Omri
   a. commander of Elah's armies
   b. reigned about 17 years
7. Ahab
   a. Omri's son
   b. wicked wife Jezebel

LESSON 8
God Cares for Elijah

I. Preparing to Read

Pointer Questions

1. What did Elijah have for his evening meal?
2. Why was the woman gathering sticks?

II. Reader

"Was it selfish for Elijah to tell the woman to give him the first bun from her scanty supplies? [It was a test of her faith in his word that there would be more.]

"What really convinced the woman that Elijah was a man of God? [the raising of her son]"

III. Workbook

Some map sources would identify the stream flowing into the Jordan from the west, nearest the Dead Sea, as the brook Cherith. Other sources would locate it in northern Gilead, as indicated in this lesson.

ANSWER KEY

A.
1. Israel
2. God lives
3. dew nor rain
4. brook
5. ravens
6. Twice
7. there was no rain
8. what Elijah said
9. brook
10. widow
11. sticks
12. handful
13. little
14. Elijah
15. till the Lord sent rain again
16. her sin

B.

3	6	14
1	9	11
4	7	15
2	8	13
5	10	12

C.
1. (Israel colored yellow)
2. Tishbe
3. (Cherith traced with blue)
4. (a line from Cherith to Zarephath)
5. (*Zidon* underlined)
6. (*Shiloh* circled)

D. (Individual pictures)

E.
1. consulted
2. chastise
3. hearkened
4. rent
5. Entreat
6. besought
7. carcass
8. sepulcher
9. cracknels
10. cruse
11. feign
12. slept

Gradebook: 50 points, counting one point for part D

LESSON 9
Elijah Talks to King Ahab

I. Preparing to Read

Pointer Questions

1. What was Ahab hunting when Elijah finally came out of hiding?
2. Why had there been no rain?

II. Reader

"Why did Obadiah think Ahab would kill him?

"Who was the one that troubled Israel? The one who was really the troublemaker wanted to blame the trouble on someone else. Sometimes we get confused just as Ahab was. Sometimes things get unpleasant for us because we have not been doing what we should. Then something makes us want to blame everyone else for the way things are going. We are mixed up when we think such things. It is believing a lie to think that we are always in the right and everyone else is wrong."

III. Workbook

ANSWER KEY

A.
1. yes
2. no
3. yes
4. no
5. no

B.
1. The famine lasted *three years.*
2. The famine had come because of *Ahab's wickedness.*
3. The *people and animals suffered.*
4. *God hid Elijah.*
5. He wanted him to gather them to *Mount Carmel.*

C.
1. feared the Lord
   men of God
2. wicked
   worshipers of Baal
   wanted to kill Elijah
3. beasts
   four legs
4. drops of water
   wet
5. necessary to live
   good
6. kings
   men
7. prophets of God
   good
8. eat
   like kind treatment
   living
9. grow
   green
10. stand upright
    have limbs
    grow
11. place to live
    entrance
12. water
    wet

D. (Possible titles)
Famines
God Provides

E. 1. Sometimes enemies took the food.
2. Many places in the world today people do not have enough.
3. It is a time when there is not enough to eat.
4. People from many countries went to Egypt for food. (or) Many places in the world today, people do not have enough.

F. 1. food
soon

2. look
brooks

LESSON 10
"The Lord, He Is the God"

I. Preparing to Read

Pointer Questions

1. What was the test that would prove who is God?
2. How many barrels of water were poured over Elijah's sacrifice?

II. Reader

Test reading comprehension with this oral quiz. Have the children write *yes* or *no* for each number.

1. Were the prophets of Baal at the contest? (yes)
2. Were the people of Israel at the contest? (yes)
3. Did Ahab give the directions for the contest? (no)
4. Did they use seven bullocks for the sacrifices? (no)
5. Did they say the one who answered by sending rain would be God? (no)
6. Did Elijah dress his bullock first? (no)
7. Did the prophets of Baal put fire under their sacrifice? (no)
8. Did the sacrifice of Baal's prophets burn? (no)
9. Did Elijah use the same altar the prophets of Baal used? (no)
10. Did Elijah put fire under his sacrifice? (no)
11. Did Elijah put water on his sacrifice? (yes)
12. Did Elijah's sacrifice burn? (yes)
13. Was it morning when God sent fire? (no)
14. Did the fire burn the stones? (yes)
15. Were the prophets of Baal killed? (yes)

Discussion

"Where do you suppose they got all the water to pour on the sacrifice in this time of no rain? [Mount Carmel was near the sea, and the sea had not dried up. Perhaps the brook Kishon was still flowing.]

"For what did Elijah pray? [He did not ask God to send fire. He asked Him to show that He was God.]"

To help the children visualize the scene, discuss the awesomeness of the fire that fell and consumed the wood, sacrifice, water, and stones.

III. Workbook

Encourage the children to print the pronunciations for part E by ear and use the glossary to verify or correct their answers.

ANSWER KEY

A.
1. c
2. c
3. a
4. a
5. c
6. b
7. a
8. a
9. c
10. a
11. a
12. b
13. b

B.
I. A. two bullocks
B. one
C. it in pieces
D. it on wood
E. no fire under it
F. your gods
G. he answers by sending fire

II. A. the bullock
B. it on wood
C. on their god, Baal
D. up and down on the altar
E. themselves with knives

III. A. come near to him
B. the altar of the Lord
C. a ditch around the altar
D. wood on the altar
E. the bullock; laid it on the wood
F. of water poured on the sacrifice
G. Lord

IV. A. fire
B. that He is God

C.
1. Rehoboam
Abijah
Asa
Jehoshaphat
2. Jeroboam
Nadab
Baasha
Elah
Zimri
Omri
Ahab

D.
1. h
2. k
3. l
4. e
5. d
6. c
7. b
8. f
9. g
10. i
11. a
12. j
13. m
14. n

E.
1. nā' dab
2. bā' ə•shə
3. jez' ə•bel
4. bā' əl
5. jē•hosh' ə•fat
6. ē' lä
7. ē•lī' jä
8. ker' ith
9. zar' ē•fath
10. ō•bə•dī' ä
11. zim' rī
12. om' ri

LESSON 11
Elijah Flees from Jezebel

I. Preparing to Read

Pointer Questions

1. What was the first sign of rain Elijah's servant saw?
2. What did Elijah eat that gave him strength for forty days?

II. Reader

"What did Jezebel say would happen if she did not kill Elijah by the next day? Did the gods kill Jezebel? Could they have killed her?

"Which prayer of Elijah's did God not answer the way Elijah asked? Why not? [God was not finished with Elijah on the earth. There were still some things for him to do.]

From where did the food come? [The angel probably placed it there.]"

III. Workbook

Consider some of the analogies in part C with the class. Have them state the relation between the first pair of words in a one sentence, keeping the words in the same order and substituting other words for *is to*. (Food *can be* cake. A tree *can be*____ . Summer *is not a time of* snow. Famine *is not a time of* _____.)

ANSWER KEY

A.
1. Mount Carmel
2. between his knees
3. rain
4. seven
5. like a man's hand
6. Elijah
7. The hand of the Lord was on him.
8. Jezebel
9. furious
10. kill Elijah
11. by the next day
12. yes

B.
1. He wanted to *get away from Jezebel.*
2. He was *tired of being hunted and having to hide.*
3. *The angel* put the food there.
4. It gave him *strength for forty days and forty nights.*
5. He *hid in a cave.*

C.
1. juniper
2. abundance
3. journey
4. chariot
5. messenger
6. wilderness
7. Horeb
8. furious

D.
1. (Lesson 8) He prayed that the widow's child would live again.
2. (Lesson 10) He prayed that God would let the people know that He is the Lord.
3. He prayed for rain.
4. He prayed that he could die.

(*X* on the number for the prayer that he might die)

E. 1. (Mount Carmel circled)
2. (line from Mount Carmel to Jezreel)
3. (line from Jezreel to Beer-sheba)
4. (line from Beer-sheba to area of Wilderness of Zin)
5. (line from wilderness to Mount Horeb)
6. forty

LESSON 12
God Speaks to Elijah

I. Preparing to Read

Pointer Questions

1. What was Elijah's reason for being at the cave?
2. What work did God yet have for Elijah?

II. Reader

"In what did God appear on the mountain? [the still, small voice]

"How was God going to punish Ahab's house? [death by Hazael, Jehu, or Elisha]

"What did Elijah do to Elisha? [threw his mantle on him]"

III. Workbook

ANSWER KEY

A.

Across	*Down*
2. earthquake	1. kiss
6. Ahab	2. Elisha
7. still	3. Horeb
8. Jehu	4. entrance
12. cave	5. Hazael
13. mantle	9. boiled
15. yoke	10. seven
17. twelve	11. small
19. fire	14. Elijah
20. die	16. oxen
21. God	18. wind
22. clothes	

B. 1. "What are you doing here, Elijah?"
2. a. The Lord was *not in the wind.*
b. The Lord was not *in the earthquake.*
c. The Lord was not *in the fire.*
3. God still had *work for him* to do.
4. Elijah was told to anoint *three* people.
5. God was getting ready to *destroy the wicked house of Ahab.*

C.

1. 19, 12	11. 13
2. 10	12. 3
3. 11	13. 5
4. 1	14. 9
5. 15	15. 4
6. 19	16. 8
7. 17	17. 11
8. 18	18. 6
9. 7	19. 14, 16
10. 2	20. 20, 11

D.

1. ov ***er***
2. w ***or*** k
3. alt ***ar*** s
4. moth ***er***
5. h ***ear*** d
6. fath ***er***
7. aft ***er***
8. ***ear*** th
9. ret ***ur*** n
10. whoev ***er***
11. c ***our*** age
12. ***ear*** thquake
13. oth ***er***
14. w ***or*** shiped
15. wild ***er*** ness

Gradebook: 68 points

LESSON 13
The Syrians Fight Against Israel

I. Preparing to Read

Pointer Questions

1. Why did Ahab say Ben-hadad could have his gold, silver, wives, and children?
2. What did the older men advise King Ahab to do?

II. Reader

"What do we mean when we say, 'Do not count your chickens before they are hatched'? One does not actually have the chickens before they are hatched. They may not hatch. They may die. One should not plan on all the benefits from something he does not actually have yet.

"When does one put on his harness? [in preparation for battle] When does one take it off? [after the battle] Ben-hadad should not have counted on winning the battle when he had not yet gone to the battle.

"Were Ahab and his people following the Lord? Why did God want to help them? [so that they, as well as the Syrians, would know that He is the Lord]"

III. Workbook

Note part C and remind the children that a sentence usually sounds better if the phrases end with nouns or verbs.

ANSWER KEY

A.

1. yes
2. no
3. no
4. no
5. no
6. no
7. yes
8. no
9. no
10. yes

B.

1. c
2. b
3. a, c, d
4. b, c
5. b
6. a
7. b
8. b (Accept *c* as well.)

C.

1. a
2. b
3. b
4. a
5. a
6. b
7. a
8. b
9. a
10. a

D.

1. h ***or*** ses
2. st ***ar*** t
3. qu ***ar*** el
4. l ***or*** d
5. f ***or***
6. h ***ar*** m
7. ***ar*** my
8. h ***ar*** ness
9. bef ***or*** e
10. l ***ar*** ge
11. L ***or*** d
12. h ***or*** semen

E.
1. i
2. f
3. h
4. b
5. a
6. c
7. j
8. g
9. d
10. e

F.
1. e
2. i
3. g
4. f
5. a
6. b
7. h
8. d
9. j
10. c

LESSON 14
The Syrians Return

I. Preparing to Read

Pointer Questions

1. Why did the Syrians think they could win the next battle?
2. How did Israel's army compare to the Syrian army?
3. Why did God help Israel this time?

II. Reader

"How was the army of Israel like two little flocks of kids? Kids have four legs and hoofs and hairy coats and bleating cries. Israel's army was not like kids in every way. Kids are little and helpless when attacked by an enemy such as a lion or a bear. In that way Israel could be compared to kids because they were not very mighty before the attacking Syrians.

"What was the reason that Israel had overcome the Syrians? [God helped them.]

"What did the Syrians think was the reason? [They assumed Israel's God was a god of the hills.]

"What promises did Ahab and Ben-hadad exchange? [to spare life and to return conquered cities]"

III. Workbook

Question 4 in part B is not directly answered in the reader. Depending on your class discussion, there may be a wide variety of correct answers.

ANSWER KEY

A.
1. hills
2. plain
3. seven
4. one hundred thousand
5. wall
6. bedroom
7. sackcloth
8. brother
9. cities
10. not pleased

B.
1. They thought Israel's God was a *god of the hills.*
2. God helped Israel to win the second battle because *the Syrians said He was God of the hills* and not of the valleys.
3. "The kings of Israel are *merciful* kings."
4. King Ahab was *merciful* to Ben-hadad.

C.
1. Elisha
2. juniper
3. comparison
4. Damascus
5. replace
6. Jehu
7. entrance
8. mantle
9. Hazael
10. Ben-hadad

D.
1. e
2. h
3. a
4. f
5. d
6. b
7. g
8. c

E. (Letters in bold print are to be circled.)
1. entr ***a*** nce
2. D ***a*** mascus
3. proph ***e*** t
4. Syri ***a*** n
5. junip ***e*** r
6. opini ***o*** n
7. heath ***e*** n
8. chari ***o*** t
9. sep ***a*** rat ***e*** d
10. serv ***a*** nts
11. c ***o*** mpar ***i*** s ***o*** n
12. valu ***a*** bl ***e***

(These answers represent glossary pronunciations. Other sources may indicate schwa for the *u* in *Damascus* and the *i* in *juniper.*)

LESSON 15
Ahab Sins More

I. Preparing to Read

Pointer Questions

1. Who was the man Ahab allowed to get away?
2. Why would Naboth not sell his vineyard?

II. Reader

"Why did the son of the prophet want to be hit? [to make his object lesson real] Often it is easier to judge the mistakes of other people than to see our own faults. The prophet's story helped Ahab to understand what he had done wrong. The prophet Nathan also used a story to help David realize what an awful thing he had done when he had Uriah killed so he could have Uriah's wife. Jesus sometimes told stories about the sins of other people to help His listeners see their own sin."

This may be an appropriate time to tell a story that has an application to some correction needed in class.

"What did Jezebel mean by saying, 'Are you not ruling the kingdom of Israel?' ["You are the king; people have to do as you say."]

"What was wicked about Jezebel's letters? [forgery, requesting unjust death]"

III. Workbook

ANSWER KEY

A.
1. true
2. false
3. false
4. true
5. false
6. false
7. true
8. false
9. true
10. false

B.
1. Ahab wanted to *make a garden* of herbs.
2. It would be handy because it was *next to his palace.*
3. He offered to give a better *vineyard or money.*
4. Naboth knew *God did not want His people to sell* what they inherited.
5. He pouted like a *naughty child* does when he cannot have his own way.

C.
1. b
2. c
3. b
4. c
5. a

D.
1. c
2. c
3. c
4. a
5. b
6. a
7. b
8. a
9. c
10. a
11. c
12. c

E.
2. first, second
3. first, second
4. second, first
5. first, second
6. first, second
7. second, first
8. second, first
9. first, second
10. second, first
11. first, second

LESSON 16
Ahab Humbles Himself

I. Preparing to Read

Pointer Questions

1. What commandments had Ahab broken?
2. What effect did the prophet's message have on Ahab?

II. Reader

"What was the real reason that Naboth died? [He upheld right against the wishes of the wicked.]

"How did God change the punishment when Ahab humbled himself? [He postponed it till the days of Ahab's son.]"

III. Workbook

ANSWER KEY

A.
1. Ahab
2. Jezebel
3. Elijah
4. Naboth
5. Jezebel
6. Elijah
7. Jezebel
8. Jezebel
9. Ahab
10. Elijah
11. Jezebel
12. Elijah

B.
1. Elijah
2. Ahab
3. Ahab
4. Ahab
5. Ahab
6. Ahab
7. Ahab
8. Ahab
9. Naboth
10. Ahab
11. Ahab
12. Ahab

C.
1. a. God b. the king
2. two
3. evil
4. covetousness
5. severe, fair
6. Jezebel
7. enemy
8. dogs
9. God
10. in Naboth's vineyard

D.
1. He was *stoned* with stones.
2. Ahab began to *think seriously.*
3. He *tore his clothes* and *dressed himself in sackcloth.*
4. God changed the punishment because *Ahab humbled himself.*
5. The punishment would not come in Ahab's days but *in his son's days.*

E.
1. c
2. a
3. d
4. b
5. a
6. c
7. b
8. d
9. b
10. d
11. c
12. a

Gradebook: 53 points

LESSON 17
Jehoshaphat, a Good King of Judah

I. Preparing to Read

Pointer Questions

1. What made Jehoshaphat's kingdom strong?
2. What mistake did Jehoshaphat make?

II. Reader

"Why would Jehoshaphat's enemies bring him presents? [They were afraid to fight him, and this would help keep him from attacking them.]

"Why was Jehoshaphat not satisfied with the answer Ahab's prophets gave? [He did not trust them and asked for a prophet of the Lord. He must have recognized that these were not of God.]

"Why do you suppose Micaiah always said evil about Ahab? [Ahab was wicked, and God's message to him was always one of judgment.]"

III. Workbook

In some areas no pronunciation difference is made between /ô/ as in *caught* and /ŏ/ as in *cot.* The phonics exercise in part E may be done by simply saying /ŏ/ for /ô/ in the directions.

ANSWER KEY

A. I. A. Judah
B. Asa

II. A. obeyed the Lord
B. follow the ways of the kings of Israel

III. A. God's laws
B. God

IV. A. fight him
B. presents

V. A. an agreement to work with Ahab
B. with Ahab in battle

B. Underline sentences 2, 3, 4, 5, 7, 8, 9, 10.

C. 1. c
2. b
3. a
4. b

D. 1. ~~sun~~, son
2. ~~besides~~, because
3. ~~bought~~, brought
4. ~~careless~~, careful
5. ~~write~~, know
6. ~~preachers~~, teachers
7. ~~word~~, world
8. ~~two~~, three
9. ~~save~~, have
10. ~~no~~, know
11. ~~two~~, four
12. ~~Ever~~, Even
13. ~~priest~~, prophet

E. 1.
2. call
3.
4. halter
5. law
6.
7. daughter
8. fault
9.
10. paw
11.
12. although
13. taught
14.
15. always
16. fall
17. also
18.
19.
20. yawn
21.
22. flaw
23.
24. altogether
25. cause
26. tall
27.
28. caught

LESSON 18
Micaiah's Word Comes True

I. Preparing to Read

Pointer Questions

1. What was Micaiah's first answer to the king?
2. What did Micaiah's second answer mean?
3. How did it happen that Ahab was wounded?

II. Reader

"What would Zedekiah see when he went into a bedroom to hide himself? [He would see that what Micaiah said was true.]

"Why did the Syrians gather around Jehoshaphat to fight with him? [They recognized him as a king by his clothes.]

III. Workbook

ANSWER KEY

A. (Most important words)
1. same thing
2. God
3. same thing
4. untruth
5. displeased
6. bad
7. to go
8. one
9. Ahab
10. Ahab came back
11. Jehoshaphat
12. only with the king
13. God
14. without trying
15. evening

B.

1. c	7. a	13. b
2. a	8. b	14. a
3. b	9. c	15. c
4. b	10. b	
5. a	11. c	
6. c	12. a	

C.
1. a. no
   b. no
   c. yes
2. a. Ahab
   b. yes
   c. yes
3. a. yes
   b. no
4. a. no
   b. yes

D. (Possible answers)
to his house
on His throne
on His right hand
in the mouth
on the cheek
into a bedroom
in prison
around him
away from the armies
to Samaria
to battle
by Him
on His left
to Micaiah
from me
to the ruler
in his robes
between the joints of the armor
into the chariot
in the pool

E.
1. right
2. fight
3. might
4. high
5. sigh
6. fright
7. tight
8. thigh
9. blight
10. nigh
11. light
12. bright

(Information to be on the kings chart)

Israel:

7. c. reigned 22 years
8. Ahaziah
   a. Ahab's son—2 years

LESSON 19
Jehoshaphat Helps His People

I. Preparing to Read

Pointer Questions

1. What must a good judge remember?
2. Who went ahead of the army to the battle?
3. Who killed the enemies?

II. Reader

Test reading comprehension with an oral quiz. Have the children write brief answers to these questions.

1. Who was the prophet that told Jehoshaphat that God was not pleased when he helped Ahab? (Jehu)
2. Where did Jehoshaphat live? (Jerusalem)
3. Would it be right to let a guilty person go without punishment if he gave money? (no)
4. How did Jehoshaphat feel when he heard the news of a great multitude coming? (afraid)
5. What did Jehoshaphat ask his people to do? (fast)
6. One of the Levites told the people not to be afraid because the battle was whose? (the Lord's)
7. When did the people leave for the wilderness of Tekoa? (the next morning)
8. What did the people in front of the army do as they went? (sang)
9. What happened to the enemies? (They fell down dead.)
10. Who was Ahaziah? (Ahab's son)
11. What did Jehoshaphat help Ahaziah to make? (ships)
12. What did God do to the things they made? (broke them)

Discussion

Locate Ammon, Moab, and Mount Seir on the map. Show En-gedi, the location of the enemy camp. Locate Tekoa and visualize the army of Judah moving from Jerusalem toward the wilderness of Tekoa, then toward Engedi the next day for battle.

"Why did the people fast? [It was a time of prayer because they were concerned about their danger. Going without food showed the greatness of their concern.]

"Why did the people worship and praise God before they even went to the battle? [God had answered their prayer with directions for them to follow and the promise that the battle was the Lord's. They trusted Him, so it was just as if the victory were already won.]"

III. Workbook

ANSWER KEY

A.
1. c
2. b
3. a
4. c
5. a
6. c
7. a
8. a
9. a
10. b
11. b
12. c
13. a
14. a

B.
1. 12, work for Judah
2. 15, joined himself to Ahaziah
3. 14, for fear the Lord would fight them
4. 7, the children of Ammon and Moab and Mount Seir
5. 8, one of the Levites
6. 10, Jehoshaphat
7. 1 or 3, Jerusalem
8. 6, fast

C.
1.
2. X
3.
4.
5. X
6.
7.
8. X

D.
1. all the kingdoms of the heathen
2. the children of Abraham
3. Israel did not destroy them.
4. a. They did not have any strength.
   b. They did not know what to do.

E.
1. Dead Sea
2. Ammon, Moab (also Edom)
3. Mount Seir
4. (Ammon, Moab, and Mount Seir colored green)
5. (En-gedi circled)
6. (line from Jerusalem to Tekoa)
7. (red spot somewhere between Tekoa and En-gedi)

F.
1. ~~w~~rong
2. ~~k~~now
3. si~~gh~~
4. ~~w~~rite
5. ti~~gh~~t
6. ~~w~~ring
7. pli~~gh~~t
8. ~~k~~not
9. ri~~gh~~t
10. ni~~gh~~t
11. ~~w~~ren
12. ~~w~~rote
13. hi~~gh~~
14. ~~k~~nob
15. ~~w~~rench
16. ~~k~~nife
17. ~~w~~reck
18. ~~k~~nee
19. ~~k~~new
20. ni~~gh~~

LESSON 20
"Is There No God in Israel?"

I. Preparing to Read

Pointer Questions

1. What did Ahaziah want to learn from a heathen idol?
2. How many men died when they went to get Elijah?

II. Reader

"How did Ahaziah know it was Elijah who had met his men? [He recognized their description. He must have known Elijah before or heard enough about him to identify him.]

"Why do you think the king sent men to bring Elijah? [Perhaps to punish him or kill him for the unwelcome message he sent to the king. If the king had been seeking to hear more of God's word, God would not have destroyed the men who came for Elijah.]"

III. Workbook

ANSWER KEY

A.

1. b	6. c	11. b
2. c	7. b	12. b
3. a	8. a	13. b
4. b	9. a	14. c
5. c	10. c	

B.

1. a, b	9. b
2. a, c	10. b, d
3. a, c	11. b, d
4. c	12. a, c
5. a, c, d	13. b, c
6. a, c	14. a
7. b, c	15. a, c
8. a, b, c	

C. (Individual work)

D.

2. became	7. found
3. sent	8. said
4. went	9. spoke
5. came	10. arose
6. told	11. made

(Information to be on the kings chart)

Judah:

4. b. reigned 25 years

Israel

9. Jehoram
   a. Ahaziah's brother

LESSON 21
Elijah Is Taken to Heaven

I. Preparing to Read

Pointer Questions

1. How did Elijah and Elisha get across the river?
2. How Elijah taken to heaven?

II. Reader

"Why was Elisha so careful to stay near Elijah? [He wanted to see him when he left so he would know that his request would be granted.]

"How did the sons of the prophets know Elisha had the spirit of Elijah? [They saw the miracle he performed to cross the river.]"

III. Workbook

The map in this lesson shows the rivers and seas without labels. You may want to drill identification in class practice.

Review the prophets' travels as mentioned in numbers 2–4 in part D so the children know to also mark the stop at Jordan and a spot across the Jordan.

ANSWER KEY

A. a chariot of fire (circled) — his clothes (double underlined)

talking (underlined) — mountain (marked x)

horses of fire (circled) — whirlwind (marked x)

mantle of Elijah (circled) — valley (marked x)

B.
1. Now
2. already
3. to
4. and
5. If
6. and
7. on
8. on
9. until
10. but

C.
1. Elijah
2. Elijah
3. Elisha
4. Elisha
5. Elijah
6. Elijah
7. Elisha
8. Elijah
9. Elisha
10. Elisha
11. Elisha
12. Elijah
13. Elijah
14. Elisha, Elijah
15. Elijah
16. Elijah
17. Elisha
18. Elijah
19. Elijah
20. Elijah
21. Elijah
22. Elijah

D.
1. (four directions printed in place)
2. (*1* beside Gilgal)
3. (*2* beside Bethel, *3* beside Jericho, *4* beside the Jordan, *5* in area across Jordan)
4. (line connecting the numbers on the map in order)
5. (all water colored blue)
6. Samaria
7. Judah
8. east

E.
1. work
2. near
3. finish
4. prophet
5. answer
6. insist
7. care
8. talk
9. sudden
10. look

LESSON 22
Elisha, the Prophet of the Lord

I. Preparing to Read

Pointer Questions

1. What was the miracle Elisha performed at Jericho?
2. Why did the children get hurt?

II. Reader

On the map given in the workbook for Lesson 19, follow the way of the kings as they went to fight Moab. "What other way could they have gone?

"Why did God give water and victory to the kings? [because the good king Jehoshaphat was with them]"

III. Workbook

ANSWER KEY

A.
1. Jericho
2. new
3. salt
4. Bethel
5. children
6. city
7. bald head
8. bears
9. woods
10. forty-two
11. Samaria
12. Moab

13. Israel
(Answers to 14–16 are interchangeable.)
14. Israel
15. Judah
16. Edom
17. seven
18. water
19. Elisha
20. Jehoshaphat
21. valley
22. ditches
23. rain
24. water

B.
1. Elisha
2. bald head
3. no
4. God
5. no
6. no
7. yes
8. no
9. yes
10. no

C. (Individual sentences. Six points in grading this exercise.)
1. *Problem:* bad water
   Action: threw in salt
   Miracle: water made good
2. *Problem:* no water
   Action: dug ditches
   Miracle: water provided

D.
1. This is a small thing for the Lord to do.
2. After that the water was always good.
3. He also will deliver the Moabites into your hand.
4. God was not pleased that they were making fun of Elisha.

(Accept logical variations, such as placing *also* at another position in the sentence.)

E.
1. pleased
2. drinking
3. coming
4. gathered
5. lived
6. worshiping
7. shining
8. chased
9. pleasant
10. caused
11. follower
12. described

Gradebook: 56 points

LESSON 23
A Widow and a Pot of Oil

I. Preparing to Read

Pointer Questions

1. Why did the widow need money?
2. What would happen if she did not get the money?

II. Reader

"From where did the oil come that filled all the vessels? [God created it as it was being poured.]

"Did that oil provide the widow with enough money to pay her debt? [Yes, there was some left over for their living.]"

III. Workbook

ANSWER KEY

A.
1. two
2. for help
3. to get the money
4. my two sons
5. a pot
6. very many
7. empty
8. from your pot
9. After they had borrowed many vessels
10. sell
11. the money that is left
12. God

B.
1. Micaiah
2. Naboth
3. Jehoshaphat
4. Ahaziah (or Jehoram)
5. Jehoram (or Ahaziah)
6. Tarshish
7. castles
8. possession
9. innocent
10. debt
11. lattice
12. vessels

C.

1	5	12
4	8	9
2	7	10
3	6	11

D.
1. de~~b~~t
2. dou~~b~~t
3. cas~~t~~les
4. lis~~t~~en
5. ~~k~~now
6. ~~k~~new
7. ~~w~~rong
8. ~~w~~rite

E.
1. in' no•cent
2. Na' both
3. Mi•cai' ah
4. Te•ko' a
5. Je•ho' ram
6. com•par' i•son
7. A•ha•zi' ah
8. Tar' shish
9. A•ra' bi•ans

LESSON 24
A Special Room and a Special Reward

I. Preparing to Read

Pointer Questions

1. What did the Shunammite woman and her husband do for Elisha?
2. Why did the woman say, "It is well" when her son had died?

II. Reader

"What would be the benefit of having Elisha speak to the king for her? [Recognition from the king would be an honor which would make most people feel important.]

"What would you answer if someone asked what you would like to have?"

III. Workbook

ANSWER KEY

A. 1. Elisha stopped at her house *whenever he passed* by that way. (*or* Elisha stopped to eat with them *when the woman invited him.*)
2. She did not want Elisha to *speak to the king for her.*
3. She had *a son.*
4. Something was wrong with *his head.*
5. He told his servant to ask *if all was well.*

B. Underline sentences 2, 4, 5, 6, 8.

C. (Picture should show a bed, table, stool, and candlestick.)

D. 1. (Shunem circled)
2. (line from Shunem to Mount Carmel)
3. (Mediterranean Sea and Dead Sea labeled)
4. (Samaria and Jerusalem labeled)
5. (line from Shunem to Gigal)
6. south

E.

1. c	6. i
2. e	7. f
3. a	8. j
4. d	9. h
5. b	10. g

F. 1. Shunammite
2. Canaanite
3. Moabite
4. Bethlehemite
5. Syrian
6. Egyptian
7. Ammonite
8. Philistine
9. Samaritan
10. Zidonian
11. Arabian

LESSON 25
Israel's Great God

I. Preparing to Read

Pointer Questions

1. What miracles with food did Elisha perform?
2. Why were the men cutting trees?

II. Reader

Test reading comprehension with this oral quiz. Have the children write *true* or *false* for each statement.

1. Elisha visited the young prophets at Gibeon. (F)
2. There was a fire where the young prophets lived. (F)
3. Elisha's servant made some soup for the sons of the prophets. (T)
4. One man put wild grapes into the soup. (F)
5. They realized the soup was poisonous. (T)
6. Elisha put some meat into the soup. (F)

7. They threw the soup away because it was poisonous. (F)
8. Someone from Shunem brought food for the prophets. (F)
9. He brought beans and barley bread. (F)
10. Elisha's servant thought it was not enough for all the people. (T)
11. The food reached around for everyone to have enough. (T)
12. There was some food left over. (T)
13. The prophets thought their place was too small for them. (T)
14. They went to build new houses at Jerusalem. (F)
15. One man fell into the water as he was working. (F)
16. Elisha threw a stick into the water. (T)

Discussion

"What did the man mean when he said, 'There is death in the pot'? [The soup was poisonous, and they would die if they ate it.]

"Who in the New Testament used a small amount of food to feed many people and had some left over? [Jesus]

"What made the ax head float? Would an ax head float if we threw a stick into the water where one had dropped in? [It was God's miraculous power that made it float and not a result of natural cause and effect.]"

III. Workbook

ANSWER KEY

A. (Most important words)
1. famine
2. servant
3. lapful
4. not
5. while
6. meal
7. in the husks
8. twenty
9. less
10. twice
11. some left
12. small
13. Jordan
14. head
15. stick

B.
1. wild
2. barley
3. borrowed
4. hungry
5. marvelous
6. surprised
7. twenty
8. big
9. young
10. fresh
11. one hundred
12. new

C. (Individual accounts of Jesus' feeding the five thousand with five loaves and two fishes)
second

D.
1. king
2. join
3. oak
4. grave
5. Abijah
6. queen
7. feet
8. brook
9. cave
10. living
11. furious
12. yoke
13. arrow
14. brother
15. dogs

E.
1. shredded
2. gotten
3. stopped
4. eating
5. tasted
6. running
7. winner
8. husked
9. thinnest
10. shutting
11. building
12. pottage

LESSON 26
A Faithful Little Slave Girl

I. Preparing to Read

Pointer Questions

1. What kind of man was Naaman?
2. Who did the king of Syria think would heal Naaman?

II. Reader

"What did the king of Israel imagine when he read the letter from the king of Syria? [He could not heal Naaman, and he was afraid the king of Syria would make war against him because he did not do what was asked.]

"What kind of treatment do you think Naaman was used to receiving? [The king of his own land looked up to him as an honorable man, so he was probably used to great honor and praise.] What was humiliating to Naaman about Elisha's treatment? [The prophet who was to heal Naaman did not even come to meet him, and washing in the muddy Jordan did not seem to be very fitting for a great man.]"

III. Workbook

ANSWER KEY

A. (Accept other reasonable wording.)

1. Naaman
2. the king of Israel
3. quarrel
4. tore
5. Elisha
6. angry
7. rivers
8. servants
9. healed
10. God

B.

1. c	4. h	7. f
2. g	5. b	8. e
3. d	6. a	9. i

C.

1. captain	7. leper
2. honorable	8. mighty
3. ~~captive~~	9. Syrian
4. brave	10. ~~king~~
5. ~~maid~~	11. master
6. ~~prophet~~	12. ~~holy~~

D.

Across	*Down*
3. Naaman	1. river
6. wicked	2. idols
9. maid	4. angry
10. leprosy	5. army
12. prophet	7. know
15. Samaria	8. wife
16. captive	11. Syria
17. letter	12. people
18. Jordan	13. help
	14. mighty
	15. seven

E.

1. 8, 9, 11, 12, 21 (Accept 10, 16, and 20 as well.)
2. 13, 14 (Accept 26 as well.)
3. 7, 17 (Accept 19 as well.)
4. 11, 23, 26 (Accept 24 as well.)
5. 4, 6 (Accept 15 and 27 as well.)
6. 130
7. 240
8. 237

9. 219
10. 140
11. "The Lord, He Is the God"
12. God Protects His People

LESSON 27
"Be Sure Your Sin Will Find You Out"

I. Preparing to Read

Pointer Questions

1. What lie did Gehazi tell Naaman?
2. What was Gehazi's punishment?

II. Reader

"How did Elisha know that Gehazi had gone to Naaman and that he lied? [God told him.]"

III. Workbook

Question 4 in part B is not answered in the story. If you included the question above in class discussion, the children should be able to give the answer.

For part E, review the rules for changing words to add suffixes.

ANSWER KEY

A.
1. yes
2. yes
3. no
4. yes
5. yes
6. yes
7. yes
8. yes
9. yes
10. yes
11. yes
12. no
13. yes
14. no
15. no
16. no

B.
1. Naaman offered money and gifts because he was *thankful for being healed.*
2. *God* had healed Naaman.
3. *Naaman's servants* carried the gifts.
4. *God told Elisha* what Gehazi had done.
5. a. Gehazi *coveted.*
   b. Gehazi *lied to Naaman.*
   c. Gehazi *lied to Elisha.*
6. He got *leprosy.*

C.
1. everything
2. lie
3. Israel
4. sin
5. homeward
6. allowed
7. God
8. Elisha
9. hid
10. after
11. Gehazi
12. is

D.
1. c
2. b
3. a
4. c
5. c

E.
1. offered
2. healing
3. promised
4. allowed
5. coming
6. believed
7. hidden
8. loaded
9. asked
10. lied
11. running
12. gotten

Gradebook: 53 points

LESSON 28
God Protects His People

I. Preparing to Read

Pointer Questions

1. Did the Lord's horses and chariots of fire fight the Syrians?
2. Who gave the Syrians a meal?

II. Reader

"How did Elisha know the plans of the king of Syria? [God told him.]

"Why did the king of Syria want to capture Elisha? [If Elisha was held prisoner or killed he could not give messages to the king of Israel.]"

III. Workbook

Questions 2, 3, and 4 in part A are not directly answered in the story. Guide the children in discussion to make these inferences.

ANSWER KEY

A.
1. c
2. a
3. b
4. a
5. b
6. c
7. c
8. b
9. b
10. c
11. c
12. a
13. b

B.

2	5	12
4	8	9
3	7	10
1	6	11

C.
1. *The Syrians* trusted in chariots and horses.
2. *Elisha* trusted in the Name of the Lord.
3. no
4. yes
5. the Lord's
6. twenty thousand
7. no
8. no
9. thousands

D.
1. paragraph 5
2. paragraph 9
3. paragraph 14
4. paragraph 2

E.
1. "Which . . . plans?"
2. "Do . . . afraid,"
3. "Lord, . . . see."
4. "Lord, . . . blind."
5. "Lord, . . . see."
6. "My . . . them?"
7. "No," answered Elisha, "you . . . them."

LESSON 29
A Terrible Famine

I. Preparing to Read

Pointer Questions

1. What had two women eaten one day?
2. What did Elisha say would happen the next day?

II. Reader

"Do you think this attack would have occurred if the king of Israel had killed the Syrians that Elisha led to him?

"How did Elisha know the king's messenger was coming and that the king wanted to kill him? [God told him.]"

III. Workbook

ANSWER KEY

A.
1. Ben-hadad
2. yes
3. Elisha
4. Elisha
5. famine

B.
1. a. The rich people paid *high prices* for only a very small amount of food.
   (or) Soon the *food was all gone.*
   b. People *ate things which are not fit to eat.*
   c. Two women *ate one of their children.*
2. a. He knew the *messenger was coming.*
   b. He knew the king was *planning to have him killed.*
   c. He knew good *food would be sold cheaply* the next day.
   d. He knew the *ruler would see it but not be able to eat any* of it.

C.
1. wicked
2. Jerusalem
3. Ahijah, Abijah
4. Levi
5. Asa
6. Elijah
7. Elisha
8. Mount Carmel

D. (Order interchangeable within numbers.)
1. a. Baasha
   b. Nadab
   c. Jeroboam
   d. Jehoram
   e. Ahaziah
   f. Ahab
   g. Jehu
2. a. Rehoboam
   b. Abijah
   c. Asa
   d. Jehoshaphat
   e. Josiah
3. a. Elisha
   b. Elijah
   c. Micaiah
   d. Ahijah
4. a. Ben-hadad
   b. Hazael

5. Jezebel
6. Naaman
7. Obadiah
8. Zarephath
9. Samaria
10. Naboth
11. Gehazi
12. Baal
13. Cherith
14. Gilgal

E. 1. d
2. f
3. c
4. e
5. h
6. a
7. g
8. j
9. b
10. i

LESSON 30
Plenty in Israel

I. Preparing to Read

Pointer Questions

1. What three choices did the lepers have?
2. What made the Syrians run away?
3. What did the king think the Syrians were planning?

II. Reader

"What convinced the people that the Syrians had actually run away? [the treasures that were dropped along the way]"

III. Workbook

ANSWER KEY

A. 1. *They would die* if they stayed sitting at the gate.
2. *They would die* if they went into the city.
3. The *Syrians might save them* alive. (or) The *Syrians might kill them.*
4. They decided to *go to the enemy camp.*

B. 1. ~~Two~~, Four
2. ~~midnight~~, twilight
3. ~~pretended~~, hired
4. ~~house~~, tent
5. ~~selfish~~, starving
6. ~~king~~, porter
7. ~~sad~~, good
8. ~~from~~, into
9. ~~grabbed~~, dropped
10. ~~smelled~~, seen

C. 1. appointed
2. captive
3. Gehazi
4. Gilgal
5. gourd
6. mistress
7. Naaman
8. pardon
9. shred
10. Shunem
11. surrounded
12. vessels

D. 1. h
2. d
3. a
4. g
5. e
6. i
7. c
8. b
9. f
10. j
11. o
12. p
13. l
14. k
15. q
16. n
17. m

TEST

ANSWER KEY

A.
1. idols
2. lion
3. idols
4. feet
5. Cherith
6. bullocks
7. fire
8. cave
9. vineyard
10. good
11. Ahaziah
12. after
13. whirlwind
14. oil
15. room
16. Gehazi
17. water
18. seven
19. lied
20. lepers

B.
1. c
2. e
3. a
4. f
5. h
6. b
7. j
8. d
9. i
10. g
11. o
12. p
13. l
14. r
15. n
16. s
17. k
18. q
19. t
20. m

C. (Any of these)
Rehoboam
Abijah
Asa
Jehoshaphat
Jehu

D. (Individual work)

Gradebook: 50 test points, giving part D 6 points value

Unit Three

Stories of the Last Kings and the Prophets

UNIT 3
General Plan

I. Preparing to Read

Suggested pointer questions are given to stimulate thinking in preparation for silent reading.

II. Reader

Suggested questions for discussion relate to thinking skills. Also continue to exercise the children in answering detail questions from things directly stated in the story.

III. Workbook

Remove and file the unit tests before distributing the workbooks.

The kings chart is continued in Unit 3. The children are required to memorize the names of the kings of Judah. Frequent oral drill will be a valuable aid. The names are given below as a source for preparing a wall chart.

You may want to encourage the children to include additional notes about the kings in the empty space on the chart in the workbook.

(Saul, David, Solomon)

1. Rehoboam
2. Abijah
3. Asa
4. Jehoshaphat
5. Jehoram
6. Ahaziah
7. Athaliah
8. Joash
9. Amaziah
10. Uzziah
11. Jotham
12. Ahaz
13. Hezekiah
14. Manasseh
15. Amon
16. Josiah
17. Jehoahaz
18. Johoiakim
19. Jehoiachin
20. Zedekiah

Unit 3 Lessons

JUDAH		ISRAEL
1. Rehoboam (1) 2. Abijah (1) 3. Asa (1) 4. Jehoshaphat (1)		
5. Jehoram (1) a. Jehoshaphat's son (1) b. reigned 8 years (1)	840 B.C.	9. Jehoram a. Ahaziah's brother b. also called Joram (1) c. reigned 12 years (1)
6. Ahaziah—Jehoram's son (1)		
7. Athaliah (4) a. Ahaziah's mother (4) b. reigned 6 years (4)	830 B.C.	10. Jehu (2) a. from another family (2) b. destroyed Ahab's house (4) c. reigned 28 years (4)
8. Joash (5) a. Ahaziah's son (5) b. became king at age 7 (5) c. reigned 40 years (6)	820 B.C. 810 B.C.	11. Jehoahaz a. Jehu's son first generation b. reigned 17 years
9. Amaziah (6) a. Joash's son (6) b. reigned 29 years (6)	800 B.C. 790 B.C.	12. Jehoash (6) a. Jehoahaz's son (6) b. second generation (6) c. reigned 16 years (6)
		13. Jeroboam a. Jehoash's son b. third generation c. reigned 41 years
10. Uzziah (7) a. Amaziah's son (7) b. became king at age 16 (7) c. became a leper (7) d. reigned 52 years (7)	780 B.C. 770 B.C.	
	760 B.C.	14. Zachariah a. Jeroboam's son b. fourth generation
		15. Shallum—another family
	750 B.C	16. Menahem a. another family b. reigned 10 years
	740 B.C.	

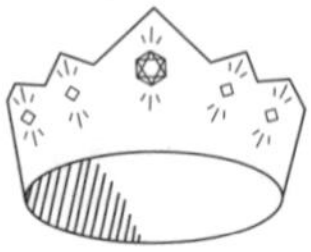

JUDAH		ISRAEL
11. Jotham (7) a. Uzziah's son (7) b. reigned 16 years (7)	730 B.C.	17. Pekahiah 18. Pekah
12. Ahaz (8) a. Jotham's son (8) b. reigned 16 years (8)	720 B.C.	
	710 B.C.	19. Hoshea (10) a. last king of Israel (10) b. reigned 9 years (10)
13. Hezekiah (8) a. Ahaz's son (8) b. reigned 29 years (8)	700 B.C.	
	690 B.C.	
14. Manasseh (13) a. Hezekiah's son (13) b. reigned 55 years (13)	680 B.C	
	670 B.C.	
	660 B.C.	
	650 B.C.	
15. Amon—Manasseh's son (13)		
16. Josiah (13) a. Amon's son (13) b. became king at age 8 (13) c. reigned 31 years (14)	640 B.C.	
	630 B.C.	
17. Jehoahaz—Josiah's son (15)		
18. Jehoiakim (15) a. Josiah's son (15) b. reigned 11 years (15)	620 B.C.	
19. Jehoiachin (24) a. Jehoiakim's son (24)	610 B.C.	
20. Zedekiah (24) a. Josiah's son (24) b. reigned 11 years (24)	600 B.C.	
	590 B.C.	

LESSON 1

The King of Israel Meets the Shunammite Woman

I. Preparing to Read

Pointer Questions

1. Why did the Shunammite woman live in the Philistines' land seven years?
2. Why did Elisha weep?

II. Reader

Perhaps someone remembers that Gehazi was smitten with leprosy and wonders how he could be allowed in the presence of the king. The king may have had an interest great enough to prompt him to summon Gehazi despite the risk.

"What else do you think Gehazi may have told the king? [He could have told about the floating ax head, the widow's oil, the multiplied food, or the healing of Naaman.]"

Point our God's perfect timing evidenced in the arrival of the Shunamite and her son while Gehazi was discussing them. God's working probably inclined the king to respond to her request favorably.

"What do you suppose the traveling prophet did with forty camels' loads of goods?" (We have no indication what he did with the goods. This question is meant to stimulate imagination.)

"Do you think that Elisha knew what would cause the death of the king of Syria? Do you think the king would have recovered if Hazael had not killed him?

"Did the people in those days think much of dogs?"

III. Workbook

For neat coloring of the map, you may want to provide pencil crayons that do not obliterate lettering.

Make sure the children know how to count paragraphs when single-line paragraphs are involved.

If the children do not have the names of the first four kings of Judah from Unit 2, you may print this list on the board for them to copy.

1. Rehoboam
2. Abijah
3. Asa
4. Jehoshaphat

ANSWER KEY

A.

1. 4
2. 10
3. 13
4. 9
5. 14
6. 12

B.

1. b
2. b
3. a
4. b
5. a
6. b
7. b
8. b
9. a
10. a

C. 2. a. The Shunammite woman and her household
b. lived
c. in the Philistines' land
d. seven years
3. a. the woman
b. At the end of seven years
c. to return to her home
d. in the land of Israel
4. a. The king
b. was talking
c. Gehazi
d. just before the Shunammite woman came to the king
5. a. The king
b. everything that was hers
c. her

D. 1. (all water colored blue)
2. (Israel colored yellow)
3. (Syria colored green)
4. (*Damascus* in Syria)
5. (Judah colored brown)
6. (Zidon colored red)
7. (Philistines' land colored purple)
8. (Ammon and Moab colored orange)
9. (*Samaria* in Israel, *Jerusalem* in Judah)
10. (*N, S, E* and *W* printed in proper place for each direction)
11. Israel
12. Syria

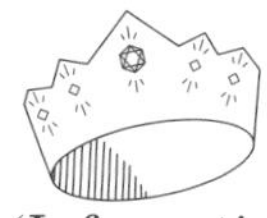

(Information to be on the kings chart)

Judah:

5. Jehoram
   a. Jehoshaphat's son
   b. reigned 8 years
6. Ahaziah—Jehoram's son

Israel:

9. b. also called Joram
   c. reigned 12 years

LESSON 2
God's Judgment on Wicked Men

I. Preparing to Read

Pointer Questions

1. How did Joram know Jehu was not coming peacefully?
2. Why did they throw Joram's body into Naboth's field?

II. Reader

A diagram on the board may help establish understanding of the family relations between characters in the two kingdoms.

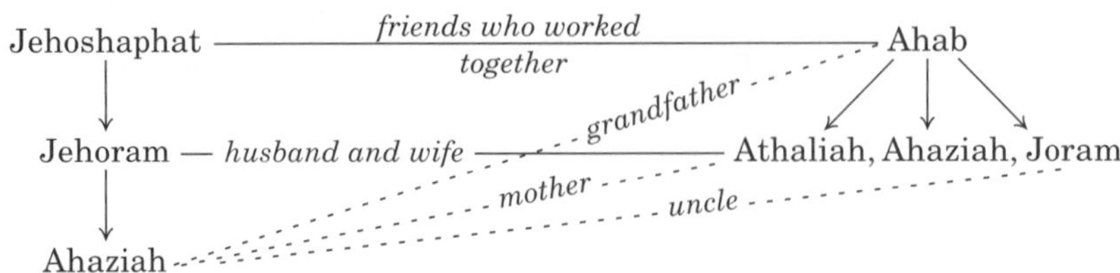

Two of Ahab's sons reigned in Israel—Ahaziah first, then Joram. Athaliah married into the kingly family of Judah. Because Joram was her brother, he was an uncle of Athaliah's son Ahaziah.

"Why was Ahaziah at Jezreel? Why was Jehu coming to Jezreel?

"What was Ahaziah's mother's name?"

III. Workbook

ANSWER KEY

A.
1. The prophet told Jehu to *destroy the whole family of Ahab.*
2. He had been *wounded in battle* with Hazael.
3. He *wanted to know if they were coming in peace.*
4. The man was *driving furiously.*
5. *Jezebel was doing such wicked things.*

B.
1. a
2. b
3. c
4. a
5. a

C.
1. b
2. f
3. c
4. e
5. a
6. d
7. h
8. g
9. i

D.
1. Hazael
2. Ahaziah
3. Jehu
4. Joram

Israel:

10. Jehu
    a. from another family

Gradebook: 25 points

LESSON 3
Ahab's Wicked House Destroyed

I. Preparing to Read

Pointer Questions

1. What happened to Jezebel's body?
2. Who killed the seventy sons of Ahab?

II. Reader

"Do you think Jehu had a kind heart? [Though he was doing God's will, his heartlessness is suggested by his command to throw Jezebel down and then by going in to eat and drink before taking thought for her burial.]

"Were the men who raised Ahab's sons on Jehu's side? What shows that they were? [their reluctance to establish a defense, their declaration of being Jehu's servants, and their prompt response in killing Ahab's sons]"

III. Workbook

Discuss the analogies in part B and do some of them with the class. Establish the relationship of the first two words and substitute the explanation for the words *is to* in the sentence. For example: Palms *are on* hands, and soles *are on* ____. Samaria *was the capital of* Israel, and Jerusalem *was the capital of* ____.

ANSWER KEY

A.
1. Jehu, Jezreel, Jezebel
2. face, floor, feet
3. seventy, sons, Samaria
4. Ahab's afraid, already
5. word, We, will, whatever
6. happen, house

B.
1. feet
2. Judah
3. cow
4. Judah
5. fence
6. body
7. arms
8. Ahaziah
9. Israel
10. wife

C.
1. yes
2. yes
3. yes
4. no
5. no
6. yes
7. yes

D.
2. praise, prays
3. maid, made
4. not, knot
5. guest, guessed
6. ate, eight
7. here, hear
8. heard, herd

LESSON 4
The Worshipers of Baal Destroyed

I. Preparing to Read

Pointer Questions

1. How did Jehu please God?
2. What was his reward?

II. Reader

"In what sense was it true that Jehu had a great sacrifice to make to Baal? [Instead of having animals killed, he had many people killed, and it was because of the idol Baal.]

"Do you suppose the boy Joash had opportunity to run and play outside from the time he was one year old until he was seven?"

Test comprehension and memory by giving this oral quiz after discussion of the story. Have the children write briefly something that each of these characters did in the story.

1. Jehu
2. Jehu's eighty men
3. Athaliah
4. Jehoiada
5. Joash

III. Workbook

ANSWER KEY

A.
1. every one
2. 80
3. 4
4. all but one
5. 28
6. 6
7. 3

B.
1. He wanted all the Baal worshipers to come *so he could kill them.*
2. There were many Baal worshipers, and they *all came.*
3. He had them put on *special clothes.*
4. The guard would *be killed* if he let a Baal worshiper escape.
5. They were all *killed.*
6. *Four generations of his sons would be kings.*
7. They would make a king's son the next king, and *she wanted to reign.*

C.
1. b
2. a
3. a
4. a
5. c
6. b
7. c
8. a

D.
1. tried
2. families
3. bodies
4. buried
5. skies
6. hurried
7. pennies
8. ladies
9. dizziness
10. laziest
11. holiness

Judah:

7. Athaliah
   a. Ahaziah's mother
   b. reigned 6 years

Israel:

10. b. destroyed Ahab's house
    c. reigned 28 years

LESSON 5
Joash, the Boy King

I. Preparing to Read

Pointer Questions

1. How was money collected to repair the temple?
2. What was done with the extra money?

II. Reader

"Why did Athaliah not like to see Joash crowned king? [She was selfish and wanted the position for herself.]

"Who actually did the ruling while Joash was young? [The priest Jehoiada was the one that made decisions and said what should be done.]

"What shows that Joash was interested in the things of the Lord? [his urgency in having money provided for repairing the temple] What shows that the people of Judah were interested in the things of the Lord? [their eagerness to contribute money]"

III. Workbook

ANSWER KEY

A. 1. b
2. d
3. e
4. c
5. a

B.

3	8	10
4	5	11
1	7	12
2	6	9

C. 1. Jezebel
2. Athaliah
3. Athaliah
4. Jezebel
5. Jezebel
6. Athaliah
7. Jezebel
8. Athaliah

D. 1. Athaliah
2. Hazael
3. Joash
4. Jehoiada
5. Ahaziah
6. Joram
7. Jezebel
8. Jehu
9. Elisha
10. Gehazi
11. The Shunammite
12. Ahab
13. Baal

E. 1. b
2. a
3. b
4. a
5. c
6. c
7. b
8. a
9. c

Judah:

8. Joash
   a. Ahaziah's son
   b. became king at age 7

LESSON 6
The Sad End of Joash

I. Preparing to Read

Pointer Questions

1. Why was Jehoiada buried with the kings?
2. What miracle happened in Elisha's grave?

II. Reader

"Whose advice did Joash follow when Jehoiada was no longer living? To whom would he not listen? [the prophets and the priest's son, Zechariah]

"Why could the small Syrian army defeat Judah?

"Why do you think Joash was not buried with the kings?

"Where was King Jehoash when he shot the arrow? Where did he shoot it? In what direction do you think Aphek was from the place where Elisha lay? [probably east]"

III. Workbook

ANSWER KEY

A.
1. yes
2. no
3. no
4. no
5. no
6. no
7. no
8. no
9. no
10. no
11. yes
12. no
13. yes
14. no
15. yes
16. no
17. yes
18. yes
19. no
20. no
21. yes
22. no
23. yes

B.
1. a
2. c
3. b
4. c
5. c
6. a
7. c

C.
1. a
2. c
3. f
4. e
5. d
6. b
7. i
8. l
9. j
10. k
11. g
12. h

Judah:

8. c. reigned 40 years
9. Amaziah
   a. Joash's son
   b. reigned 29 years

Israel:

12. Jehoash
   a. Jehoahaz's son
   b. second generation
   c. reigned 16 years

D.
1. Rehoboam
2. Abijah
3. Asa
4. Jehoshaphat
5. Jehoram
6. Ahaziah
7. Athaliah
8. Joash
9. Amaziah

E. (Individual attainment)

Gradebook: 60 points, counting one point for part E

LESSON 7
Uzziah and Isaiah

I. Preparing to Read

Pointer Questions

1. What did Uzziah do that was sinful?
2. What made Isaiah feel sinful?

II. Reader

"Who was the prophet that helped Uzziah to obey God? [This is not the same Zechariah mentioned in Lesson 6 who was stoned.]

"Why do you think so many priests were very concerned about what Uzziah was doing? [They realized the seriousness of disobeying the Lord in the sacred things of the temple. The Lord had already struck people dead for doing things differently from what He designed.]

"Describe the heavenly beings Isaiah saw. [They had six wings, and faces, feet, and hands.]

"What did Isaiah prophesy, about seven hundred years before it took place?"

III. Workbook

ANSWER KEY

A. 1. young great X proud

X angry helped by God

X disobedient X leprous

2. Sentences to be crossed out are b, c, d, f, j, k, l.
3. Holy, holy, holy, earth
4. send

B.

1.	when	11.	where
2.	when	12.	when
3.	where	13.	when
4.	when	14.	where
5.	where	15.	where
6.	why	16.	why
7.	why	17.	where
8.	when	18.	where
9.	where	19.	where
10.	why	20.	why

C.

1.	b	8.	b	15.	b
2.	a	9.	b	16.	b
3.	c	10.	a	17.	a
4.	c	11.	b	18.	c
5.	b	12.	a	19.	b
6.	a	13.	c	20.	c
7.	a	14.	a	21.	a

D.

1.	pities	9.	glorying
2.	pitied	10.	drier
3.	pitying	11.	driest
4.	buries	12.	drying
5.	buried	13.	spied
6.	burying	14.	spies
7.	glories	15.	spying
8.	glorious		

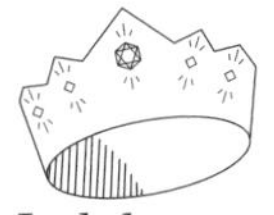

Judah:

10. Uzziah
    a. Amaziah's son
    b. became king at age 16
    c. became a leper
    d. reigned 52 years
11. Jotham
    a. Uzziah's son
    b. reigned 16 years

E. 1.

4	1	11
5	3	8
2	10	7
6	9	

LESSON 8
Ahaz and Hezekiah

I. Preparing to Read

Pointer Questions

1. How did the people of Israel treat their captives from Judah?
2. What project did Hezekiah start as soon as he became king?

II. Reader

"What two kings worked together to punish Judah?

"What two reasons did the prophet give that Israel should not keep captives from Judah? [Israel also deserved punishment, and the men of Judah were their brothers.] Why did the prophet say the people of Judah were brothers to the people of Israel? [They were all of the same family in that they descended from Abraham, Isaac, and Jacob. Israel and Judah were considered together as a nation of God's people.]

"Why did Ahaz think the gods of the Syrians helped them? [Syria with Israel had overcome Judah, but it was because God wanted to punish Judah and not because the Syrian gods had any power.]"

III. Workbook

Give some practice in oral pronunciation of the words in part C.

ANSWER KEY

A.

1. H
2. A
3. A
4. H
5. A
6. H
7. A
8. A
9. H
10. A
11. H
12. A
13. H

B.

1. *Ahaz was a very wicked king.*
2. The people of Judah were *brothers* to Israel.
3. He *thought the gods of the Syrians helped* them.
4. a. They were to *stand before the Lord.*
   b. They were to *serve the Lord.*
   c. They were to *burn incense.*
5. They *sanctified themselves.*
6. They took the dirt to the *brook Kidron.*
7. They finished cleaning in *16 days.*

C.

1. witch
2. which
3. Wine
4. whine
5. whale
6. wail
7. where
8. wear
9. wheel
10. We'll

D. wonderful, willing

Judah:

12. Ahaz
    a. Jotham's son
    b. reigned 16 years
13. Hezekiah
    a. Ahaz's son
    b. reigned 29 years

E. 1. Rehoboam
2. Abijah
3. Asa
4. Jehoshaphat
5. Jehoram
6. Ahaziah
7. Athaliah
8. Joash
9. Amaziah
10. Uzziah
11. Jotham
12. Ahaz
13. Hezekiah

LESSON 9
Judah Worships the Lord

I. Preparing to Read

Pointer Questions

1. What did Hezekiah want all the people of Israel and Judah do?
2. At what times did the people rejoice?

II. Reader

"Who brought the animals for the sin offering? How many animals were there?

"Who brought the animals for the sacrifices and thank offerings? How many were there that time? [so many that the priests needed extra help to handle them]

"What did Hezekiah promise would happen if the people would turn to the Lord?

"What was the response to Hezekiah's letter in the two kingdoms?"

III. Workbook

Discuss wording answers to say exactly what a question asks. You may want to do some of exercise B with the class.

ANSWER KEY

A. I. A. 1. Seven bullocks
2. Seven rams
3. Seven lambs
4. Seven he goats

B. 1. Killed them
2. the blood
3. it on the altar

II. A. 1. to sing the song of the Lord.
2. worshiped God.
3. were blown

B. 1. bowed their heads and worshiped.
2. sang psalms and praises.
3. bowed their heads and worshipped.
4. sacrifices and thank offerings.
5. rejoiced.

B. 1. b
2. a
3. c
4. a
5. c
6. a
7. b

C. 1. f
2. b
3. c
4. a
5. d
6. e
7. l
8. j
9. g
10. h
11. k
12. i

D.

2. al/tar
3. com/mand
4. let/ters
5. car/ry
6. in/vite
7. stub/born
8. cap/tive
9. en/ter
10. af/ter
11. al/low
12. don/keys
13. fol/low
14. hap/pened
15. Kid/ron
16. ves/sels
17. en/gines
18. in/cense
19. hur/ried
20. fif/ty

E.

6	4	12
2	3	11
5	13	10
1	8	9
7		

LESSON 10
Trouble in Israel

I. Preparing to Read

Pointer Questions

1. Was Hoshea a good king?
2. Why did the king of Assyria think he could destroy Jerusalem?

II. Reader

"What was the reason that Israel would no longer be a nation? What happened that ended the nation of Israel?

"What did Hezekiah do to keep the king of Assyria from taking Jerusalem?

"How did the people respond to Rabshakeh's threats?"

III. Workbook

ANSWER KEY

A.

1. 19
2. None
3. Assyria
4. after
5. temple
6. Jerusalem
7. weak
8. Jews
9. afraid
10. Hezekiah
11. did not
12. king

B.

1. Rehoboam
2. Abijah
3. Asa
4. Jehoshaphat
5. Jehoram
6. Ahaziah
7. Athaliah
8. Joash
9. Amaziah
10. Uzziah
11. Jotham
12. Ahaz
13. Hezekiah

C.

1. d
2. j
3. e
4. a
5. f
6. b
7. i
8. c
9. g
10. h

D.

1. wor/***sh*** ip
2. fol/low
3. or/***ph*** an
4. far/***th*** er
5. mas/ter
6. ki ***ng***/dom
7. pur/pose
8. al/***ph*** a
9. un/der
10. ri ***ng***/let
11. mar/***sh*** al
12. pil/lar
13. ker/***ch*** ief
14. per/suade
15. pan/***th*** er
16. ques/tions

Israel:

19. Hoshea
    a. last king of Israel
    b. reigned 9 years

Gradebook: 54 points for the entire lesson, counting one point for each word in part D

LESSON 11
The Proud Assyrians Are Destroyed

I. Preparing to Read

Pointer Questions

1. When did Hezekiah want Isaiah to pray for the people?
2. When did Hezekiah himself pray?

II. Reader

Have the children write short answers for this oral quiz to test comprehension after silent reading.

1. How many men did the king send out to talk with Rabshakeh? (three)
2. Who was the king of Judah at this time? (Hezekiah)
3. What did the king do to his clothes when the men told him what Rabshakeh had said? (tore)
4. Who said the king should not be afraid of the army? (Isaiah / the Lord)
5. From what land was Rabshakeh? (Assyria)
6. What did the king spread before the Lord? (the letter)
7. What had the Assyrians done to the gods of other nations? (destroyed them)
8. Who promised to defend Jerusalem (God)
9. Who killed the people in the enemy camp? (the angel of the Lord)
10. How many were killed? (185,000)

Discussion

"What would it prove to all nations if they saw the Assyrians destroyed while trying to take Jerusalem? [The Lord is the true and living God and not just another idol as the gods of the other nations.]"

III. Workbook

ANSWER KEY

A.

1. no	5. no	9. no
2. no	6. no	10. yes
3. no	7. yes	11. no
4. no	8. no	12. no

B.
1. *None of the other gods had saved* their nations.
2. They had *destroyed* them.

C.
1. He is the God of *all the kingdoms* of the earth.
2. He made *heaven and earth.*
3. They were *no gods.* (or) They were *wood and stone.*
4. He wanted God to save them so everyone would *know that He is God.*

D.
1. Rehoboam
2. Abijah
3. Asa
4. Jehoshaphat
5. Jehoram
6. Ahaziah
7. Athaliah
8. Joash
9. Amaziah
10. Uzziah
11. Jotham
12. Ahaz
13. Hezekiah

E.
1. looked
2. farming
3. useless
4. carry
5. proud
6. came near
7. prophet
8. completely

LESSON 12
Hezekiah's Last Days

I. Preparing to Read

Pointer Questions

1. What was the sign that Hezekiah would be healed?
2. How did Hezekiah show that he was proud after he was healed?

II. Reader

"What might Hezekiah have done to set his house in order? [organize business matters to leave no confusion for others who would take over his affairs] What did he do instead? [He turned to the wall and prayed for dear life.]

"Did the lump of figs heal the king? [We do not know that the figs had any medical value. God healed him in answer to his prayer.]

"What makes the shadow on a sundial? What makes it go forward?

"Why was Hezekiah honored at death? What good had he done? [He opened the temple and restored true worship in Judah.]"

III. Workbook

You may want to provide red pencil crayons for part D. Have the children do number 1 in class as a sample, underlining just the key words *pride* and *fall*. You may want to do some additional numbers in class as well.

ANSWER KEY

A.

2	8	12	19
1	7	14	16
5	6	15	18
4	9	13	20
3	10	11	17

B. 1. b
2. a

C. 1. c
2. e
3. d
4. a
5. b
6. f

D. (Answers may vary in length. Key words are given here.)

Red

1. Pride
2. became proud,
showed the men from Babylon all his treasures,
boasted
3. boasted of his greatness,
said God could not save Jerusalem
4. "Who is the Lord that I should obey Him?"
wanted his own way
5. make a name for themselves,
wanted to be great people

Black

1. fall
2. carry away all his treasures
3. killed all the king's captains and great men
4. terrible plagues,
drowned in the Red Sea
5. confused their speech,
scattered to many places of the earth

E. 1. Ahab
2. Ahaz
3. Jotham
4. Joram
5. Abijah
6. Ahijah
7. Elijah
8. Elisha
9. though
10. through
11. appointed
12. anointed
13. bought
14. brought

F. 1. Rehoboam
2. Abijah
3. Asa
4. Jehoshaphat
5. Jehoram
6. Ahaziah
7. Athaliah
8. Joash
9. Amaziah
10. Uzziah
11. Jotham
12. Ahaz
13. Hezekiah

LESSON 13
God's Judgment and Mercy

I. Preparing to Read

Pointer Questions

1. How did the Lord bring judgment on Manasseh?
2. How did the Lord show mercy to Manasseh?

II. Reader

"How could God wipe Jerusalem as a man wipes a dish? [A dish that is wiped and turned upside-down would surely have nothing in it. God would so thoroughly destroy the city there would be nothing left there.]

"What made Manasseh think of the Lord? [He was in trouble and needed someone greater than himself to turn to for help.]

"What kind of punishment came upon Amon?"

III. Workbook

ANSWER KEY

A.
1. c
2. d
3. f
4. a
5. e
6. b
7. l
8. j
9. g
10. k
11. h
12. i

B. (Order interchangeable)
1. He built *altars to Baalim.*
2. He made his *children pass through fire.*
3. He used *witchcraft.*
4. He *made his people do wicked things.*
5. He *killed innocent people.*
6. He *made an idol* and set it up in the temple.
7. He *did not heed the warning* of the prophets.

C. (Order interchangeable)
1. He *took away the idols.*
2. He *got rid of the altars* he had built.
3. He *repaired the altar of the Lord.*
4. He *sacrificed to the Lord.*
5. He *commanded Judah to serve the Lord.*

D.
2. pass
3. name
4. sent
5. evil
6. Israel
7. depart
8. more
9. own
10. was

E.
3. i/dol
4. Da/vid
5. Ju/dah
6. pun/ish
7. e/vil
8. o/bey
9. Am/on
10. ru/mor
11. nev/er
12. shad/ow
13. pres/ent
14. cov/er
15. A/sa
16. heav/en
17. rea/son
18. vis/it

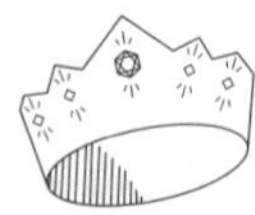

Judah:

14. Manasseh
    a. Hezekiah's son
    b. reigned 55 years
15. Amon—Manasseh's son
16. Josiah
    a. Amon's son
    b. became king at age 8

LESSON 14
The Good Reign of Josiah

I. Preparing to Read

Pointer Questions

1. How was the Book of the Law found?
2. What did the king and the people promise?

II. Reader

"What kind of 'cleaning' did Josiah do in Judah and Jerusalem? [a moral cleaning of removing idolatry]

"Why did King Josiah tear his clothes upon hearing the Book of the Law read?

"Where did Josiah clean up besides Jerusalem and Judah?

III. Workbook

Do some examples in part C with the children in class.

ANSWER KEY

A.
1. 2 (twenty years old)
2. 3 (the high priest)
3. 5 (Josiah had obeyed the Lord.)
4. 6 (the priests, the prophets, and all the people)
5. 7 (They would obey the words in the Book.)
6. 9 (The men of the city told him.)
7. 11 (the Passover)

B.
1. c
2. a
3. a
4. b

C.
1. b, c
2. c, d
3. b, d
4. a, c
5. c, d
6. b, c
7. a, b
8. c, d
9. a, b
10. b, c
11. c, d
12. b, c
13. a, c
14. b, c
15. b, c
16. a, b
17. c, d
18. a, d

D.

7	2	12
4	3	10
8	13	11
6	9	15
5	16	14
1		

E. (Bold letters are to be circled.)
1. Be ***th*** /el
2. hea/***th*** en
3. wi ***ck*** /ed
4. pro ***ph*** /ets
5. Jo/***th*** am
6. o ***th*** /er
7. ne ***ph*** /ew
8. cu ***sh*** /ion
9. ei/***th*** er
10. mo ***th*** /er
11. Na/***th*** an
12. no ***th*** /ing

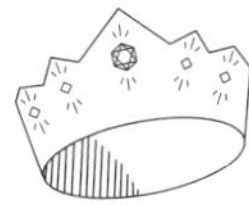

Judah:

16. c. reigned 31 years

LESSON 15
Daniel Dares to Do Right

I. Preparing to Read

Pointer Questions

1. Who took Johoahaz captive, and where did he take him?
2. Who took Jehoiakim captive, and where did he take him?

II. Reader

"What did the Jews have to learn before they could be helpful in Nebuchadnezzar's kingdom?

"What was wrong with the king's wine and meat? How would they defile Daniel? [The defilement would be spiritual. It would be sin for him to disobey God's commands.]

"Does a diet of vegetables and water make people wiser? [Healthy eating habits will have an effect on mental abilities, but this was more than that. The wisdom of Daniel and his friends was a gift from God; He blessed them for their obedience.]"

III. Workbook

Discuss the change in map scales. Notice the smallness of the Dead Sea, Jordan River and Canaan area which often constituted the complete map in workbook exercises. Help the children realize that if those areas were as big as usual, the rest of the map would be so much bigger, indicating the great distance to Babylon.

ANSWER KEY

A.
1. (line from Jerusalem to Babylon)
2. (*EAST, SOUTH,* and *WEST* printed in correct place. Three points in grading.)
3. east
4. Euphrates

B.

1. C	6. C
2. C	7. C
3. H	8. H
4. H	9. C
5. H	10. C

C.
1. a. The captives *could not speak his language.*
   b. He *chose wise, healthy young people* who could learn the language.
2. a. He was given *wine and meat that God did not want* His people to drink and eat.
   b. He *asked one of the princes to excuse him* from eating these things.
3. a. If they did what Daniel wanted they might be *killed for not following the king's orders.*
   b. They agreed to a *ten-day test* to see how a different diet would work.

D. 1. laws
2. determined
3. the way God wanted him to be
4. God
5. polite
6. the prince
7. healthier
8. wisdom
9. ten

E. 1. Hoshea
2 Nebuchadnezzar
3. Chaldeans
4. Manasseh
5. Jehoahaz, Jehoiakim
6. Rabshakeh
7. Babylon, Melzar
8. diet
9. defile
10. rumor
11. sundial
12. fulfilled, prophecy

F. (Oral)

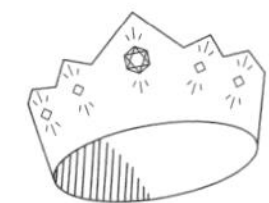

Judah:
17. Jehoahaz—Josiah's son
18. Jehoiakim
a. Josiah's son
b. reigned 11 years

Gradebook: 56 points for all written work, counting two points for sentence answers

LESSON 16
The Wise Men of Babylon in Danger

I. Preparing to Read

Pointer Questions

1. What did the king want his wise men to tell him?
2. How did Daniel find out what the king had dreamed?

II. Reader

"Why did a captain come to kill Daniel?

"Did Daniel think he could figure out what the king had dreamed when he asked the king for time? [No, he knew God would have to help him.]

"Were the other wise men of Babylon killed?"

III. Workbook

ANSWER KEY

A. 1. c
2. c
3. b
4. b
5. c
6. c
7. c
8. a
9. c

B. 1. yes
2. the Lord
3. for ever and ever
4. wisdom, might
5. wisdom, might
6. a. times, seasons
b. kings, sets them up
c. wisdom, knowledge
d. secret things

C. 1. a
2. b
3. b
4. a
5. a
6. a
7. b
8. b

D. 1. Rehoboam
2. Abijah
3. Asa
4. Jehoshaphat
5. Jehoram
6. Ahaziah
7. Athaliah
8. Joash
9. Amaziah
10. Uzziah
11. Jotham
12. Ahaz
13. Hezekiah
14. Manasseh
15. Amon
16. Josiah
17. Jehoahaz
18. Jehoiakim

E. 1. Mel/zar
per/chance
wor/ship
ac/cuse
ex/cept
2. trea/son
sea/sons
Me/shach
hea/then
Ki/shon
3. cov/et
bish/op
tal/ents
neph/ew
cab/in

LESSON 17
Nebuchadnezzar's Dream

I. Preparing to Read

Pointer Questions

1. What did the image in the king's dream represent?
2. Whom did King Nebuchadnezzar worship?

II. Reader

"Did Nebuchadnezzar know whether the things Daniel said were in the dream he had forgotten?

"Why was Daniel made ruler over all the wise men? Why were Shadrach, Meshach, and Abednego made rulers?"

III. Workbook

ANSWER KEY

A. 2. (great)
11. (bright)
14. (terrible)
1. (gold)
4. (silver)
5. (brass)
7. (iron)
7. (iron) } interchangeable
10. (clay) }
12. (stone)
13. (mountain)
8. (feet)
3. (chaff)
9. (wind)
12. (stone)
13. (mountain)
6. (earth)

B.
1. c
2. d
3. e
4. b
5. a

C.
(yellow)
(white)
(orange)
(gray)
(gray and brown)

D.
1. among
2. heaven
3. never
4. break
5. many
6. Babylon
7. future
8. revealer
9. friends
10. glory

E.
1. head
2. face
3. arms
4. thighs
5. breast
6. feet
7. belly
8. hands
9. legs

F.
1. Rehoboam
2. Abijah
3. Asa
4. Jehoshaphat
5. Jehoram
6. Ahaziah
7. Athaliah
8. Joash
9. Amaziah
10. Uzziah
11. Jotham
12. Ahaz
13. Hezekiah
14. Manasseh
15. Amon
16. Josiah
17. Jehoahaz
18. Jehoiakim

LESSON 18
Three Men Who Would Not Bow

I. Preparing to Read

Pointer Questions

1. Who was at King Nebuchadnezzar's celebration?
2. What was the signal for everyone to bow before the image?

II. Reader

Test comprehension after silent reading with this *true/false* quiz.

1. Nebuchadnezzar's image was made of gold, silver, brass, iron, and clay. (false)
2. He put his image on a great mountain. (false)
3. Nebuchadnezzar called all his rulers to a celebration. (true)
4. Shadrach, Meshach, and Abednego came to the celebration. (true)
5. The people were supposed to bow when the herald talked. (false)

6. Every one of the rulers bowed down to the image. (false)
7. Three Chaldeans stayed standing when the others bowed. (false)
8. Nebuchadnezzar was furious that some people disobeyed him. (true)
9. Nebuchadnezzar offered to give Shadrach, Meshach, and Abednego, another chance to bow. (true)
10. Nebuchadnezzar said, "Who is that God who can deliver you out of my hands?" (true)
11. Shadrach, Meshach, and Abednego were afraid of the king. (false)
12. They knew that God would deliver them from the king. (true)

III. Workbook

Not all the words for exercise A appear in the story. Numbers 2 and 5 must be answered by rewording the thought from the story.

Part D may be simplified by an oral review. Give each item as a question and let the children mark the number with *yes* or *no.*

ANSWER KEY

A.
1. feet
2. front
3. fall
4. fiery furnace
5. feared
6. fell
7. forever
8. from
9. furious
10. for

B.

4	9
5	6
2	8
1	10
3	7

C.
1. To set free from evil or danger
2. "And who is that God who can deliver you out of my hands?"
3. a. who can deliver us from the burning fiery furnace."
   b. deliver us out of your hand, O King."

D. Nebuchadnezzar

E.

1. gold/en	6. great/er
2. burn/ing	7. fear/less
3. bold/ly	8. tall/est
4. bow/ing	9. plant/ed
5. law/ful	10. dust/y

LESSON 19
Three Men Who Would Not Burn

I. Preparing to Read

Pointer Questions

1. What did Nebuchadnezzar see in the furnace that was hard to believe?
2. What burned in the fire?

II. Reader

"Why was the king furious in Lesson 18? [Three men dared to disobey him.] What made him furious at the beginning of this lesson? What loss did the king have because of his fury? [The most mighty men in his army died, probably just because of the unnecessarily multiplied heat. Anger makes people think and do unreasonable things that only result in damage.]

"What did Nebuchadnezzar call God? [the Most High God, the God of Shadrach, Meshach, and Abednego]

"What word of the king did the three men change? [Nebuchadnezzar had boldly spoken against God. Now he said that anyone who spoke against God should be cut into pieces. There was no question that his speech changed from making himself great to declaring God's greatness.]"

III. Workbook

Note that a few of the words at the end of exercise D should be divided into more than two syllables by applying previously studied syllabication rules.

ANSWER KEY

A.
1. c
2. b
3. a
4. b
5. a
6. c

B.

Across	*Down*
1. flames	2. scorched
3. Meshach	3. most
7. furious	4. singed
9. furnace	5. hair
10. seven	6. bodies
12. ropes	7. four
14. smell	8. serve
15. fire	11. no
16. burn	13. even
17. bind	14. Son

C. (Individual work)

D.
1. un/true
2. a/round
3. a/rose
4. re/turn
5. fore/told
6. a/wake
7. pre/cooked
8. dis/o/bey
9. im/per/fect
10. un/faith/ful

LESSON 20
Nebuchadnezzar Dreams Again

I. Preparing to Read

Pointer Questions

1. What did Nebuchadnezzar dream?
2. How long did Daniel think about the dream before he told the king what it meant?

II. Reader

"Why did Nebuchadnezzar write his letter? Whose wonders and signs and kingdom did he praise?

"What part of the dream do you think would have made Nebuchadnezzar afraid even though he did not know what it meant? [The destruction of the great tree may have struck fear to his heart.]

"Why do you think Daniel was troubled and wondered what to do? [He would have to tell the king some very unpleasant things when he explained the meaning of the dream.]"

III. Workbook

ANSWER KEY

A. (The description and picture should include these points.)
- high tree
- animals
- birds
- fruit

B. (The description and picture should include these points.)
- cut down
- leaves gone
- fruit scattered
- animals and birds gone
- stump remaining

C.
1. c
2. a
3. a
4. b
5. b

D.
1. men
2. gods / one
3. God
4. signs / tree / king
5. wonders
6. kingdom
7. tree
8. heart
9. years
10. God

E.

8	3	11
7	2	16
6	1	10
5	14	13
9	15	18
4	17	12

LESSON 21
The Dream Comes True

I. Preparing to Read

Pointer Questions

1. In what ways was Nebuchadnezzar like an animal?
2. Whom was Nebuchadnezzar praising in paragraph 2? in paragraph 8?

II. Reader

"What does the sentence mean that says Nebuchadnezzar's palace grounds were beautiful? [The lawns, gardens, shrubs, flowers, and whatever surrounded his palace were beautiful. Babylon was the site of the famous hanging gardens, which had plants on platforms above luxurious rooms.]

"Who rules in the kingdom of men? To whom does He give the kingdom? How did Nebuchadnezzar come to be in the position of king? [God decided to have him rule and could decide whenever He pleased to remove him. There was no real greatness or power in Nebuchadnezzar himself.]"

The content in this story except for the last paragraph was also included in the letter Nebuchadnezzar wrote to all people of the earth.

III. Workbook

Discuss the statements in part A to help the children understand what details in the story give a basis for making the statements.

ANSWER KEY

A.
1. 1
2. 1, 2, or 4
3. 3
4. 4
5. 5
6. 5
7. 6
8. 6
9. 7
10. 7

B.
1. Daniel, determined, stand
2. defile, eat
3. excused, rest
4. three, king, ten, everything
5. troubled, sleep, day
6. wise, all
7. king, time
8. pray, secret, know
9. plain, image, bow, fire
10. delivered, God, He

C.
1. treas/ure
2. sher/iffs
3. her/ald
4. re/vealed
5. de/file
6. fur/nace
7. coun/sel/or
8. re/veal/er
9. hast/y
10. sus/pect/ed

LESSON 22
The Lord Speaks to Jeremiah

I. Preparing to Read

Pointer Questions

1. What kind of messages did God want Jeremiah to give?
2. What did Pashur do to Jeremiah?

II. Reader

The scene switches from Babylon to Judah. The last stories dealt with the captives taken to Babylon. Now we read about the corresponding years in Judah, where some of the people remained.

"Did Jeremiah really wish his head was water? [He was very much grieved about the sinful condition of the people and their refusal to repent. One can naturally weep only so long until the tears are spent. This was Jeremiah's way of expressing his continued grief, when he had no more tears to shed.]

"What effect did the messages of the false prophets have? [They gave the people hope for peace without repentance.] Why did God want His people to hear the unpleasant messages? [He loved them, and He wanted them to repent so He could bless them.]"

III. Workbook

ANSWER KEY

A. (No written work)

B.
1. S (Judah)
2. R
3. S (did not feel able)
4. R
5. R
6. S (false)
7. R
8. R
9. S (felt sorry)
10. S (Weeping Prophet)
11. S (Book of Lamentations)
12. S (put him into prison)
13. R
14. R
15. R

C. A summary is a *short* report that tells the *main thoughts.*

D.
1. e
2. c
3. a
4. j
5. f
6. k
7. b
8. i
9. d
10. h
11. g

E.
1. c
2. b
3. c
4. b

F.
1. Rehoboam
2. Abijah
3. Asa
4. Jehoshaphat
5. Jehoram
6. Ahaziah
7. Athaliah
8. Joash
9. Amaziah
10. Uzziah
11. Jotham
12. Ahaz
13. Hezekiah
14. Manasseh
15. Amon
16. Josiah
17. Jehoahaz
18. Jehoiakim

Gradebook: 50 points

LESSON 23
Jeremiah Warns the People

I. Preparing to Read

Pointer Questions

1. In what way was Jeremiah brave?
2. What did the father of the Rechabites command his family?

II. Reader

"What do you think were the bad things against the temple that the priests and prophets blamed Jeremiah for saying? [He told of destruction that would come as punishment.]

"Who respected Jeremiah's message as from the Lord?

"Why did the people of Judah not respond to Jeremiah's message? [They wanted to continue in sin rather than repent.] Why did the Rechabites not do as Jeremiah told them? [They were determined to faithfully obey their father.]"

III. Workbook

ANSWER KEY

A.
1. stand
2. in the court of the Lord's house
3. every word that God commanded
4. might
5. not punish them
6. did not like
7. The priests and prophets
8. sat
9. The older men
10. through the prophets
11. did not bring evil on them
12. to drink wine
13. The Lord
14. to show how obedient they were
15. everything
16. always
17. pleased

B.
1. Jeremiah had *said evil* things would happen to them and the temple.
2. Jeremiah had *spoken in the Name of the Lord.*
3. a. They were not to *drink wine.*
   b. They were not to *build houses.*
   c. They were not to *sow seed.*
   d. They were not to *plant vineyards.*
4. They were to *live in tents.*
5. They *obeyed their father* in everything.

C.
2. 3, 1, 2
3. 3, 2, 1
4. 2, 3, 4, 1

D.
1. proph/ets
2. be/cause
3. fol/low
4. for/sook
5. what/ev/er
6. in/no/cent
7. mis/treat/ed
8. re/mind/ed
9. pun/ish/ment
10. at/ten/tion
11. un/kind/ly
12. to/geth/er

LESSON 24
The King Tries to Destroy God's Word

I. Preparing to Read

Pointer Questions

1. Who wrote the words in the book?
2. How many people believed God's Word when Baruch read it?

II. Reader

Test comprehension and memory with this oral quiz. Have the children write the word for the blank in each sentence.

1. God wanted Jeremiah to write all the words of His message in a ____. (book *or* roll)
2. God gave these messages so that people would turn back to Him and He could ____ them. (forgive)
3. Jeremiah said the words of God's messages, and ____ wrote them down. (Baruch)
4. Jeremiah sent Baruch to the ____ to read the words of the Lord. (house of the Lord / temple.)
5. Baruch read the book on the ____ day. (fast)
6. One man reported to the ____ what he had heard. (princes)
7. The princes wanted the ____ to hear the words in the book. (king)
8. The princes thought Jeremiah and Baruch should ____ themselves. (hide)
9. The king was in his ____ house. (winter)
10. The king cut off some pages with a ____. (knife)
11. He threw them into the ____. (fire)
12. The second book was longer than the first because it told about the punishment of ____. (Jehoiakim)

Discussion

"What did Jeremiah mean when he said he was shut up? [He was not allowed to speak in the temple.]

"What is a fast day?"

Discuss the family relation of the last four kings. Jehoahaz, Jehoiakim, and Zedekiah were all Josiah's sons.

III. Workbook

Some of the information for part D is not in the reader but can be found on the kings chart.

ANSWER KEY

A. 1. "It may be that when they hear about the evil that I plan to do to them, they will come back to Me. *Then I can forgive their sin."*

2. *"Do not let any man know where you are."*

3. *The Lord hid them.*

B. 2
1
5
3
4

C.

1. c	3. a	5. b
2. c	4. a	6. b

D. 1. Jehoiakim
2. Jehoiachin
3. Jehoiakim
4. Jehoiachin
5. Jehoiakim
6. Jehoiakim
7. Jehoiakim

E. 1. the Lord
2. Israel
3. Judah
4. Jeremiah
5. Pashur
6. Jehoiakim
7. the priests and prophets
8. the princes
9. the Rechabites
10. Baruch
11. the princes
12. Jehoiakim
13. the false prophets
14. the king's servant

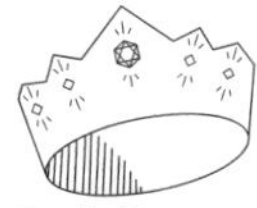

Judah:
19. Jehoiachin
  a. Jehoiakim's son
20. Zedekiah
  a. Josiah's son
  b. reigned 11 years

F. (Oral exercise)

LESSON 25
Judah's Punishment

I. Preparing to Read

Pointer Questions

1. Who said that things would be well for the captives taken to Babylon?
2. Who said God had broken the yoke of Babylon?

II. Reader

"What object lessons did God use to help Jeremiah or others to understand His messages? [figs and wooden yokes]

"How was Hananiah punished for giving a false message?"

III. Workbook

ANSWER KEY

A.	B.	C.			
1. c	1. b	1. e	6. i	11. l	16. o
2. a	2. a	2. c	7. d	12. n	17. k
3. e	3. b	3. g	8. f	13. p	18. r
4. f		4. a	9. b	14. t	19. m
5. b		5. j	10. h	15. s	20. q
6. d					

D.

1. Amon	1. Amon
2. Josiah	2. Josiah
3. Jehoahaz	3. Jehoahaz
4. Jehoiakim	4. Jehoiakim
5. Jehoiachin	5. Jehoiachin
6. Zedekiah	6. Zedekiah

E.

3. āmen	11. cănnot
4. thăt	12. lănd
5. băd	13. fămine
6. sāy	14. tāken
7. cărried	15. băck
8. māke	16. nātions
9. căptive	17. Bāruch
10. plănt	18. Băbylon

LESSON 26
Jeremiah Writes to the Captives

I. Preparing to Read

Pointer Questions

1. How long would the captives be in Babylon?
2. Why were the princes angry with Jeremiah?

II. Reader

"Is it a likely thing that wounded men would be able to take a city? [God was sending His judgment, and it was His will that Jerusalem be taken. It was that sure, that even if the Jews had managed to wound all the Chaldeans, they would still take the city.]

"Why did Zedekiah call for Jeremiah? Why do you think he wanted to keep his business secret? [Perhaps he was afraid to let others know that he was interested in Jeremiah's messages. Zedekiah was a man who feared what others thought, as shown in the following lessons.]

"What else did Jeremiah talk to the king about, besides God's message?"

III. Workbook

ANSWER KEY

A.

1. no	6. no
2. yes	7. no
3. no	8. no
4. yes	9. no
5. yes	10. yes

B. (The letter should include these points.)

Plan to stay.
Build houses.
Plant gardens.
Get married.
Pray for the city.
Beware of false prophets.
Return after seventy years.

C.

1. d	7. g
2. i	8. f
3. k	9. a
4. j	10. h
5. b	11. c
6. l	12. e

D.

1. tōld, Gŏd
2. stāy, hăve
3. lĭst, līed

4. ēat, lĕt
5. rāised, găther
6. trŭst, cūre
7. prĭson, fīght
8. drēams, hĕlp
9. prāy, lănd
10. whĭch, tīme
11. pēace, lĕft
12. ōnly, nŏt

Gradebook: 56 points, counting 10 points for part B and 2 points for each number in D

LESSON 27
Ebed-melech Helps Jeremiah

I. Preparing to Read

Pointer Questions

1. What was it like in the dungeon where Jeremiah was placed?
2. Why did Zedekiah not want to follow Jeremiah's advice?

II. Reader

"What things did Jeremiah know before they happened? [His uncle's son was coming. The Jews would live if they surrendered to the Chaldeans and die if they stayed in the city.]

"What was Jeremiah's advice to the people? Why did the princes think that was not good advice? [It went against their reasoning to think it would be better for them to give themselves into the hands of their enemies.]

"What did the princes ask of the king? [Jeremiah's death] What did they do to cause Jeremiah's death? [They put him in a dungeon.]

"What did Jeremiah want the king to promise? [that the king would not have him put to death and that he would heed Jeremiah's advice] Which promise did the king make? [not to have Jeremiah put to death]"

III. Workbook

ANSWER KEY

A.
1. They should *give themselves to the Chaldeans.*
2. They thought he was *saying things for the hurt of the people.*
3. They *cast him into a dungeon.*
4. (Individual answer) He probably asked for a message from God.

B.
1. cousin
2. money
3. die
4. black *or* brown
5. friend

C.
1. a prophet in Judah
2. king of Judah
3. which cannot be eaten
4. a false prophet
5. into which they were taken
6. which have come to help you
7. an Ethiopian
8. I beg of you

D. 1. l	8. d	**E.** 1. b	
2. e	9. j	2. a	
3. k	10. b	3. a	
4. a	11. i	4. a	
5. h	12. g	5. b	
6. c	13. m		
7. f			

LESSON 28
Jerusalem Is Taken by the Chaldeans

I. Preparing to Read

Pointer Questions

1. How did the Chaldeans get into the city?
2. Who burned the houses of Jerusalem?

II. Reader

"What did the princes ask Jeremiah? What did Jeremiah answer?

"What did the people do when the Chaldeans came? What were they trying to avoid? [slavery] What suffering did they bring on themselves instead? [hunger]

"What did the Chaldean captain understand about the destruction of Jerusalem? [He knew the Chaldeans had been able to take the city because the Jews had disobeyed the Lord.]

"What did Jeremiah choose to do? Who else was also at Jerusalem? [the poor and those the Chaldeans did not desire as captives; Gedaliah, who was made their governor]"

III. Workbook

ANSWER KEY

A.	B.	C.	
1. c	1. e	1. Rehoboam	11. Jotham
2. e	2. d	2. Abijah	12. Ahaz
3. f	3. c	3. Asa	13. Hezekiah
4. b	4. b	4. Jehoshaphat	14. Manasseh
5. a	5. g	5. Jehoram	15. Amon
6. d	6. f	6. Ahaziah	16. Josiah
7. g	7. a	7. Athaliah	17. Jehoahaz
8. h		8. Joash	18. Jehoiakim
9. i		9. Amaziah	19. Jehoiachin
10. j		10. Uzziah	20. Zedekiah

D.
1. kind
2. cruel
3. thankful
4. determined
5. temper
6. faith
7. proud
8. loved
9. coward
10. curious

E.
1. ă
2. ā
3. ä
4. ă
5. ô
6. ä
7. ä
8. ā
9. ô
10. ă
11. ô
12. ä

LESSON 29
Ishmael Deceives Gedaliah

I. Preparing to Read

Pointer Questions

1. Who understood Ishmael's wicked intentions?
2. Why did the people not know about Gedaliah's death for several days?

II. Reader

"What points indicate that Gedaliah was a good governor? [He told the people not to be afraid to serve the Chaldeans, which harmonized with Jeremiah's message. He assured the people it would go well for them to live in the land. He gave direction to gathering provisions. He trusted people—perhaps too much.]

"Why did Ishmael not kill ten of the eighty men who came? [He spared them for the treasures they brought, which indicates the value he placed on riches.]

"Who rescued the captives from Ishmael?"

III. Workbook

ANSWER KEY

A.
- I. A. gathered to him.
  - B. returned to Jerusalem
  - D. all the people who were left
- II. A. serve the Chaldeans
  - B. in the land
  - C. wine and summer fruits
- III. A. Ishmael had been sent to kill him.
  - B. kill Ishmael.
- IV. A. Gedaliah
  - B. the Jews and the men of war with him
  - C. most of the eighty men who came with offerings.

B.
1. 6
2. 3
3. 3
4. 8

C.
1. Pashur
2. Johanan
3. Ebed-melech
4. Nebuzaradan
5. Belshazzar
6. Zedekiah
7. Baruch
8. Gedaliah
9. Hilkiah

D. (Individual work)

LESSON 30
The People Go to Egypt

I. Preparing to Read

Pointer Questions

1. For what was Jeremiah to pray?
2. What was the answer?

II. Reader

"What did Johanan and the people think would be the best thing to do? What did they do to make sure their idea was right?

"The people said, 'Whether it is good or evil, we will obey the Lord.' Did they think God might tell them to do something evil? [They would call evil something like captivity or some other hardship such as the punishment God sent on Jerusalem. They were saying they would take God's way even if it was something unpleasant to endure.]

"Did they obey the voice of the Lord?

"What became of Jeremiah? [The Jews took him along to Egypt. The Bible does not say what happened to him there. Some people think the Jews stoned him in Egypt. Some people think that when the Chaldeans overcame Egypt, Jeremiah went to Babylon, where he died in peace.]"

III. Workbook

Most of the names in part C are glossary entries. The children should do as many of the sentences as they can by memory before using the glossary as a resource.

ANSWER KEY

A.
1. They were afraid to stay because *Ishmael had killed their governor.*
2. They wanted Jeremiah to pray about *what they should do.*
3. Jeremiah waited *ten days* for the Lord's answer.
4. God wanted them *to stay* in their land.

B.
1. c
2. b
3. a
4. a
5. c
6. b
7. a
8. b
9. a
10. c

C. (Possible answers)

2. was Elisha's servant.
3. was a Hebrew captive in Babylon
4. was a good king of Judah
5. was a false prophet (or) was one of Daniel's friends.
6. was a good priest who helped King Joash.
7. were Hebrew captives who would not bow to Nebuchadnezzar's image.
8. was the Weeping Prophet in Judah.
9. was a wicked queen in Judah.
10. was a king of Syria

11. was the king of Judah who burned God's Word.
12. was a prophet of the Lord who did many miracles.
13. was a prophet who saw a vision of God's throne.

D. (Individual work)

TEST

ANSWER KEY

A.
1. e
2. i
3. n
4. j
5. b
6. h
7. c
8. a
9. l
10. m
11. f
12. k
13. d
14. g

B.
1. false
2. true
3. false
4. false
5. true
6. true
7. false
8. true
9. false
10. true
11. true
12. true

C.
1. Babylon
2. image
3. gold
4. tree
5. animal
6. kingdoms
7. prayer
8. Judah
9. Assyria
10. shoot
11. night
12. angel
13. captains

D.
1. Rehoboam
2. Abijah
3. Asa
4. Jehoshaphat
5. Jehoram
6. Ahaziah
7. Athaliah
8. Joash
9. Amaziah
10. Uzziah
11. Jotham
12. Ahaz
13. Hezekiah
14. Manasseh
15. Amon
16. Josiah
17. Jehoahaz
18. Jehoiakim
19. Jehoiachin
20. Zedekiah

Gradebook: 59 test points

Unit Four

God's People During and After the Captivity

UNIT 4
General Plan

I. Preparing to Read

Two pointer questions are given with each lesson to stimulate thinking before silent reading. They may be discussed orally or written on the board as an assignment. Be sure to include any assigned pointer questions in oral discussion following reading.

II. Reader

Some deeper thought questions are given for oral discussion, but do not limit your discussion to these. Ask *who, what, when,* and *where* questions which can easily be formulated right in class.

III. Workbook

After silent and oral reading, encourage independence in doing workbook exercises without referring to the reader. Frequently direct the children to go through the lesson and do all they can without the reader. Let them circle the numbers of the questions they were able to do on their own and then use the reader to find the others. Pay attention to the number of *correct* circled items, rather than just noting how many were circled.

Remove and file the unit tests before distributing the workbooks.

Unit 4 Lessons

LESSON 1
Ezekiel's Visions

I. Preparing to Read

Pointer Questions

1. What did God want Ezekiel to eat?
2. What would happen to the dry bones?

II. Reader

A few paragraphs in the story end with multiple quotation marks. Write a sample sentence on the board to explain their use.

The minister explained, "Jesus said, I have not found such faith in all Israel as this woman who said, The dogs eat of the crumbs from the master's table."

Point out that everything within the quotation marks was spoken by the minister. He told of something Jesus said. Within the minister's quote we use single quotation marks to show what Jesus said to avoid confusion with the signs that show the minister is speaking. Place the single quotation marks and note that Jesus' words also end at the end of the minister's sentence. Jesus' words also included a quotation of someone else. To mark the words of the woman, we use another set of double quotation marks inside the marks that show Jesus' words. Place these marks, noting that her words are also at the end of the sentence, which puts all three quotation marks on a pile.

"Why had the Jews been punished and taken captive to other lands? [because of their idolatry]

"What was the meaning of the bones coming together and coming to life? [The Jews had been taken captive and scattered in many lands. In a sense their nation was dead. God was promising to bring them back to the land of Israel again. The bones were gathered together into bodies and became alive as a sign that God would gather the Jews to the land of Israel again.]

"Was God talking about literal graves in the last paragraph? [He was referring to the many lands in which the living Jews were "buried" or held captive.]"

III. Workbook

ANSWER KEY

A.
1. b, c
2. c
3. a, c, d
4. c
5. a, b, c, e
6. a
7. b
8. c
9. b, c
10. b

B. (Possible answers; any four)

He saw beautiful visions of God.

He ate a roll of a book

He saw visions of idolatry in Jerusalem.

He was carried to the middle of a valley.

Dry bones came together to form skeletons.

The dead bodies came to life.

C. (Individual work)

D.
1. no
2. yes
3. yes
4. yes
5. yes
6. yes
7. no
8. yes
9. yes

(Make allowance for a child's reasoning that produces answer variations, since these are "What do you think" questions.)

LESSON 2
Belshazzar Sees a Fearful Sight

I. Preparing to Read

Pointer Questions

1. What were the lords?
2. What did Belshazzar do with the vessels from the temple?

II. Reader

"What had happened to Nebuchadnezzar when he become proud?

"Why do you think the king and the wise men could not read what was written on the wall? [It was probably written in another language, perhaps Hebrew, the language of God's people.]

"How did the queen describe Daniel?"

III. Workbook

ANSWER KEY

A.
1. a, b
2. a, c
3. a, b, c
4. none
5. b, c
6. a
7. b, c
8. a, b, c
9. none
10. a, b, c

B.
3. wine
4. gold and silver
5. Fingers
6. terrified / troubled
7. wise
8. scarlet
9. gold
10. the third
11. The queen
12. Judah
13. prophet / priest
14. Babylon
15. a roll / a book
16. woes
17. tie Ezekiel up
18. the sun
19. in the middle of
20. an army

C.
1. He knew *what had happened to Nebuchadnezzar* when he became proud.
2. He *did not take warning.*
3. Fingers of a man's *hand wrote on the wall.*
4. His *face changed,* and his *knees hit* against each other.
5. The *queen* was sure that Daniel could tell the meaning.

6. She knew about his wisdom *in Nebuchadnezzar's day.*

7. Daniel *did not want* the king's rewards.

LESSON 3
Trouble in Babylon

I. Preparing to Read

Pointer Questions

1. What trouble was in Babylon?
2. Why did King Darius like Daniel?

II. Reader

"Note the difference in Daniel's attitude from the time he interpreted the dream for Nebuchadnezzar. He accused King Belshazzar. When King Nebuchadnezzar dreamed, Daniel kept troubled silence an hour and then said he wished the interpretation to the king's enemies. Why? [Belshazzar had Nebuchadnezzar's experience as an example and knew better. Also, he was desecrating God's property by using the temple vessels as he did.]

"What does 'weighed and found wanting' mean? [Measured or judged and found with a lack. Belshazzar was not what he should have been in obedience.]"

"Do you think Belshazzar liked the message Daniel gave? Do you think he believed it? How did he treat Daniel?

"Did Daniel become the third ruler in Belshazzar's kingdom? [Belshazzar's kingdom was ended that night.] In whose kingdom did Daniel have a very high place?

"What would be the good of a law like the one the princes proposed to the king? [not much more than to inflate the ego of the king and make the people think of the king as God]"

III. Workbook

ANSWER KEY

A.
1. God
2. when he became proud
3. he wanted to
4. a. humbled his heart
   b. glorified God
5. that night
6. Median
7. elderly
8. 120
9. three
10. Daniel

B.
1. They were to *help in the affairs* of the whole kingdom. (or) They were to *report to the presidents* what went on.
2. They did not like that *Daniel was given the highest place and was liked better* than they.
3. They tried to find fault *in the way Daniel ruled* in the kingdom.

4. He would rather *disobey the king than disobey God.*
5. King Darius signed the writing, not knowing that it was intended to be a trap for Daniel.

C.

1. a	7. a
2. a	8. b
3. c	9. a
4. b	10. c
5. c	11. a
6. b	

D.

1. no	7. yes
2. yes	8. no
3. yes	9. yes
4. no	10. yes
5. yes	11. no
6. no	12. yes

LESSON 4
Daniel in the Lion's Den

I. Preparing to Read

Pointer Questions

1. Did Daniel know what could happen to him before he went to pray?
2. What did the king say when Daniel was thrown into the lion's den?

II. Reader

"Why did the rulers say, 'That Daniel, who is of the children of the captives of Judah,' instead of saying, 'Daniel, who is the highest of the presidents'? [They did not like Daniel and wanted to make him look as despised as they could.]

"If the king knew that the law of the Medes and Persians could not be changed, why did he try to think of a way to save Daniel? [He loved Daniel. Perhaps he thought there could be an exception on the basis of the lie told him when the rulers proposed the law.]

"How could the king have avoided this problem? [by thinking things over carefully and not signing something that was purely for his own exaltation]

"The king referred to God as 'Your God, whom you serve all the time.' Did Daniel serve God when he was away from his land in a strange kingdom? Did he serve God when it was against the law? When he might die for it?"

III. Workbook

Plan an opportunity for oral reading of the sentences in part B, either when you discuss and assign the lesson or, preferably, after the lesson is done.

ANSWER KEY

A. I. A. in his house (or) in his bedroom (or) before his window
B. on his knees
C. Jerusalem
D. God
E. three
F. 1. thanks
2. requests

II. A. all the time
B. signed
C. attention

III. A. angel
B. shut

C. cuts, bruises, scratches
D. believed in his God

IV. A. all the people of the earth
B. tremble and fear
C. 1. living and steadfast
2. shall not be destroyed
3. shall be to the end
4. delivers and rescues
5. signs and wonders
6. Daniel from the power of the lions

B. 1. the princes
2. the king
3. the princes
4. the princes
5. the king
6. the king
7. Daniel
8. Daniel
9. Ezekiel

C. 1. d
2. f
3. a
4. b
5. g
6. c
7. e
8. h

D. 1. i
2. b
3. l
4. k
5. h
6. a
7. e
8. d
9. j
10. f
11. c
12. g

LESSON 5
The Return to Jerusalem

I. Preparing to Read

Pointer Questions

1. Who had prophesied that the Jews would return to their own land? (Jeremiah; also Ezekiel by the vision of the dry bones)
2. What was given to the Jews going to Jerusalem?

II. Reader

"What made Cyrus want the Jews to build the temple? What made some of the Jews get ready to go, but not all? [God worked in their hearts.]

"Why did the people offer burnt offerings and keep the feasts? [These things were commanded in God's Law.]"

On a globe, identify the extent of the Persian kingdom. Was that really *all* the kingdoms of the earth? There is much more land in the earth, but Cyrus had conquered all the kings that he knew about.

III. Workbook

ANSWER KEY

A. (The correct word is given for each answer.)
1. Persian
2. desire
3. Jeremiah
4. all
5. build
6. to the workers

7. Jerusalem
8. many
9. donkeys
10. an altar
11. burnt
12. Moses
13. Lord
14. start
15. Cedar
16. the same
17. twenty
18. sang
19. wept
20. noise

B.
1. Nebuchadnezzar
2. Darius
3. Cyrus
4. Belshazzar
5. Darius
6. Cyrus
7. Darius
8. Nebuchadnezzar
9. Belshazzar
10. Nebuchadnezzar
11. Cyrus
12. Belshazzar
13. Nebuchadnezzar
14. Belshazzar
15. Belshazzar
16. Cyrus
17. Nebuchadnezzar

C.
1. a
2. b
3. b
4. a
5. b
6. a
7. b
8. a
9. a

D.
1. (all seas and Persian Gulf, blue)
2. (*Jerusalem* circled)
3. (*Shushan* circled)
4. (all land inside heavy dotted line, yellow)

Gradebook: 50 points

LESSON 6
Enemies Hinder the Work

I. Preparing to Read

Pointer Questions

1. What did the enemies do because they did not want the temple built?
2. Who commanded that the building should be stopped?

II. Reader

"What do you think would have happened if the Jews had accepted the enemies' offer to help in the building?

"To which river might the men have been referring in their letter to the king? Consider the map in Lesson 5 in the workbook. [Euphrates or Jordan. Probably they were referring to the Euphrates, as that is a more major river and the one the king would surely think of without a name given to determine which river.]

"Why did the enemies wait until Artaxerxes was king to accuse the Jews? [They knew Cyrus wanted the temple built.]

"When was rebellion found in Jerusalem? [Before Judah was taken captive, the prophet Jeremiah advised the people to give themselves to the Chaldeans, but they resisted. They rebelled against the king of Babylon instead of serving him.]"

III. Workbook

ANSWER KEY

A.

4	9	14
1	6	11
3	8	15
2	7	12
5	10	13

B. (Order interchangeable within each numbered section)

I. A. By pretending to be friends
   B. By hindering the work
   C. By accusing them to the king
   D. By forcing them to quit working

II. A. Not paying taxes
   B. Being rebellious
   C. Bringing damage to the kings

III. A. Would not let them fool them
   B. Did not allow them to help

C. 1. a. rebuild
   b. enemies, friends
   c. temple

2. a. fool
   b. fool, knew, true, you, to (occurs five times), do, together
   c. king of Persia

3. a. hindered
   b. hard

4. a. Your servants / the men on this side of the river
   b. 1) rebellious
      2) bad

5. a. at such a time
   b. until I give further commandment

LESSON 7
The Temple Is Finished

I. Preparing to Read

Pointer Questions

1. What got the people to take up the building of the temple again?
2. What did some men do in hopes of making the Jews stop their building?

II. Reader

"Who was the other King Darius we read about before this one? [the Median who ruled immediately after Babylon's fall]

"What was different about the letter these men wrote to the king from the letter that had been written to Artaxerxes? [The men who wrote to Artaxerxes said the Jews were building the walls when they were building the temple. They declared without any proof that the Jews would rebel and not pay taxes. They did not mention the fact that Cyrus had wanted the temple built. The men who wrote to Darius were fair in telling what the

Jews said about Cyrus' command. They honestly asked the king to tell them what he desired in the matter.]

"Why did Darius want the men to let the Jews build the temple? [He found record that Cyrus had commanded it to be built. He wanted the Jews to offer sacrifices and pray for him.]"

III. Workbook

Have the children make some sample questions in class as a help for doing part B. First choose a statement from the story; then word the statement in question form to be answered with *yes* or *no.*

ANSWER KEY

A. 1. *God helped* the Jews so that the enemies could not make them stop.
2. They hoped the *king would command the Jews to stop building.*
3. a. He wanted them to *offer sacrifices* to God.
   b. He wanted them to *pray for the king and his sons.*
4. It was very *dangerous to disobey* the king.

B. (Individual work)

C.

1. c	4. d	7. b
2. g	5. h	8. a
3. i	6. e	9. f

D. (Words interchangeable within each group)

1.	2.	3.
shoes	cups	corn
dress	pan	nuts
gown	bowl	honey
coat	platter	raisins
shirt	vase	berries
hat	jar	manna

E.

1. d	6. b
2. a	7. c
3. e	8. f
4. g	9. h
5. i	

LESSON 8
The Story of Esther—Part 1

I. Preparing to Read

Pointer Questions

1. Why did the king want Vashti to come?
2. What was so serious about Vashti's refusal to come when the king called her?

II. Reader

Test the children's comprehension with this oral quiz before discussing the story. Have the children number a paper from 1 to 10 and write the correct word from the choice given in each sentence. If spelling is a problem, letter the choices *a* and *b*, and let the children write the correct letter.

1. Did Ahasuerus have his palace at *(a) Sushan* or (b) Jerusalem?
2. Was the feast held in the (a) court of the temple or *(b) court of the garden?*
3. Were the decorations *(a) white, green, and blue* or (b) red, blue, and purple?
4. Were the guests given (a) milk or *(b) wine* to drink?
5. Did Vashti invite the women from the house of (a) the prophets or the house of *(b) the king*?
6. Did the king want to show the people Vashti's *(a) beauty* or her (b) wisdom?
7. Was the king angry because Vashti (a) came to him or *(b) would not come*?
8. Did (a) the king or *(b) one of the princes* suggest that Vashti should no longer be queen?
9. Was the commandment supposed to make all the women honor (a) the king or *(b) their husbands*?
10. Were the women brought to the king's house for him to choose *(a) a queen* or (b) a servant?

Discussion

"Was Vashti a beautiful queen? Why do you think so?

"How do you think the king would show the riches of his glorious kingdom? [by displaying wealth] How do you think he would show the honor of his majesty? [perhaps by telling how people honored and praised and obeyed him]

"What did the prince mean when he said, 'Give her place to someone better than she'? [Let someone better be the queen."]"

III. Workbook

You may want to do the questions in part A orally, changing them to yes / no questions. Let the children jot *yes* or *no* beside each number and then later do the exercise, following the directions of each number marked *yes*.

ANSWER KEY

A. Shushan the Palace

B.

1. X	6.
2.	7.
3.	8. X
4. X	9. X
5. X	10. X

C. 1. c
2. a
3. b

D.

1. e	6. i
2. h	7. g
3. a	8. c
4. j	9. d
5. f	10. b

LESSON 9
The Story of Esther—Part 2

I. Preparing to Read

Pointer Questions

1. Why was Esther taken to the king's house?
2. Why did Mordecai tell what the two doorkeepers were planning to do?

II. Reader

"What does it mean to say Esther gave the message to the king in Mordecai's name? [She gave it as a message from Mordecai.]

Did Mordecai disobey the commandment to bow to Haman because he did not have any respect for the king? [No, his intervention in the plot to kill the king is evidence of his respect for the king. There must have been some other purpose for refusing to bow. As a faithful Jew, he would have been familiar with God's commandments about worship.]"

III. Workbook

ANSWER KEY

A.
1. d
2. f
3. b
4. h
5. g
6. c
7. e
8. a

B.
1. Benjamin
2. first cousin
3. yes
4. at the king's gate
5. a year
6. Jewess
7. two
8. the king's

C.
1. *Esther's parents had died.*
2. Esther was a *beautiful* lady.
3. The king *loved Esther* more than any of the other women.
4. He wanted to *know what would happen to Esther.*
5. *Mordecai had commanded her not to tell.*
6. The *king had commanded* his servants to bow to Haman.

D.
1. no
2. yes
3. yes
4. no
5. no
6. no
7. yes

E. (Accept reasonable variations.)
1. and
2. because
3. that
4. as
5. when
6. but
7. for
8. so
9. and
10. because

Gradebook: 45 points, counting two points for each sentence answer

LESSON 10
The Story of Esther—Part 3

I. Preparing to Read

Pointer Questions

1. What law of the king was not being kept by the Jews?
2. What perplexed the city of Shushan?

II. Reader

"Would King Ahasuerus likely have been living at this time if it had not been for a Jew? [Remember the doorkeepers' plot.]

"Haman said the Jews' laws were different. Whose laws did the Jews keep? [God's laws]

"What would make a writing into a law that could not be changed? [The king's special sign would have been carved or molded into his ring. Letters were sealed with wax, and if the sign on the king's ring was pressed into the wax, it would make a mark to show that this message was from the king.]

"Why do you think Esther did not want Mordecai to dress in sackcloth? [Sackcloth indicated sadness. She did not want him to be sad and to be kept out of the king's gate.]

"What did Mordecai mean when he said, 'Who knows but that you have come to the kingdom for such a time as this?' [Perhaps God had caused her to be made queen because He knew this was going to happen and He wanted to use her to save her people."

III. Workbook

ANSWER KEY

A.
1. the king
2. the scribes
3. Haman
4. all the people in the kingdom
5. sat down to drink
6. a. tore his clothes
   b. put on sackcloth with ashes
   c. went to the middle of the city
   d. cried loudly and bitterly
7. fasted with weeping and wailing (also, many lay in sackcloth and ashes)
8. He wanted Esther to *go to the king* and ask him to save the lives of her people.
9. thirty days
10. Anyone who came to the king without being called *might be put to death.*
11. yes

B.
1. no
2. no
3. no
4. no
5. no

C. perplexed
cried
loudly and bitterly
weeping and wailing
sackcloth and ashes
tore his clothes
grieved

D.

1. B	6. B	11. C	16. A
2. A	7. C	12. C	17. B
3. B	8. A	13. B	18. A
4. C	9. A	14. C	19. B
5. C	10. B	15. A	20. C

LESSON 11
The Story of Esther—Part 4

I. Preparing to Read

Pointer Questions

1. Why did the Jews in Shushan fast?
2. For what did Esther ask when she went before the king?

II. Reader

"What was the danger of going to the king without being called?

"Why did the king ask Esther at the banquet what her request was? [He was sure she wanted something more than to just invite him to a banquet. There was something important enough to make her risk her life for it.]

"What did Esther mean when she said, 'Come to the banquet tomorrow. Then I will do as the king has said'? [Then I will tell the king what I want."]"

III. Workbook

Provide opportunity for oral reading of the sentences in part C.

ANSWER KEY

A.
1. fasted
2. royal
3. inner
4. scepter
5. top
6. banquet
7. delighted / important
8. Mordecai
9. insulted
10. friends
11. gallows
12. seventy-five

B.

1. c	5. c
2. a	6. b
3. b	7. c
4. a	8. b

C.
1. questioning
2. willing and determined
3. requesting
4. boastful
5. hateful
6. cruel
7. questioning
8. commanding

D. (Individual work)

LESSON 12
The Story of Esther—Part 5

I. Preparing to Read

Pointer Questions

1. Why was Haman in the king's court that morning?
2. Why was the king wanting to honor Mordecai?

II. Reader

"Can you think of anything that might have made the king unable to sleep that night? [God may have kept him awake so he would hear the record of Mordecai's good deed and want him honored instead of killed. Perhaps the king could not sleep because he was trying to figure out what Esther could want.]

"Who did Haman say should lead the man the king wanted to honor through the city? Who was one of the king's most noble princes?

"Did the king have any idea what Haman wanted to do to Mordecai? Can you imagine how Haman must have felt when the king told him what to do?

"Why did Haman cover his head on the way home? [He felt so bad about what he had been made to do.] Why did other people cover Haman's face at the banquet? [They probably realized Haman would die.]"

III. Workbook

ANSWER KEY

A.
1. The king *had someone read to him.*
2. Mordecai had *saved the king's life* when two men wanted to kill him.
3. He was going *to ask to have Mordecai hanged.*
4. He *thought he would be honored,* and that is what he would have liked for himself.
5. a. He covered his head *after he honored Mordecai.*
   b. His face was covered *when the king spoke* at the banquet.
6. He was *hanged* on the gallows he had made for Mordecai.

B.
1. 1
2. 2
3. 2
4. 1
5. 1
6. 2
7. 1
8. 2
9. 2
10. 1
11. 1
12. 2
13. 1
14. 2
15. 1
16. 2

C.
1. b
2. d
3. a
4. c

D.
1. true
2. false
3. false
4. true
5. false
6. true
7. false
8. false
9. false
10. true

LESSON 13
The Story of Esther—Part 6

I. Preparing to Read

Pointer Questions

1. How did they make sure everyone heard about the new law?
2. What did the Jews call the feast in memory of this time?

II. Reader

"What was the house of Haman? [the position and responsibilities that had been Haman's]

"If Haman was dead, why did Esther risk her life to come to the king again? [The letters Haman had written in the king's name were still in effect.]

"What was done to keep Haman's plan from being carried out? [A new law was made, giving the Jews permission to kill anyone who tried to hurt them.]"

Check if your calendar indicates the feast of Purim, which falls in February or March of our year. The beginning of the Jewish year was reckoned from spring, so the twelfth month would be at the end of winter instead of December.

III. Workbook

ANSWER KEY

A.
1. no
2. yes
3. yes
4. no
5. no
6. no
7. yes
8. yes
9. no
10. yes
11. yes
12. yes
13. no

B. (Possible answers)
1. All Jews—men, women and children—are to be killed on the thirteenth day of the twelfth month.
2. The Jews may kill anyone who tries to hurt them on the thirteenth day of the twelfth month.

C. (Possible answers)

Hold a feast every year on the fourteenth and fifteenth days of the twelfth month. Send things to each other, give gifts to the poor, and feast with joy and gladness because God gave us victory over our enemies.

D.
1. palace, city (interchangeable)
2. Vashti, Esther (interchangeable)
3. honor, shame
4. sorrow, joy
5. gallows
6. ring, Haman
7. scepter
8. feast
9. kind, Jews
10. peace

E.
1. Ezekiel
   Zechariah
   Haggai
   Daniel

2. Belshazzar
   Cyrus
   Vashti
   Esther
   Ahasuerus
   Darius
3. innocent
   kind
   rebellious
   terrified
   great
   perplexed
   angry
   important
   proud
   wicked
4. Mordecai

Gradebook: 54 points, counting two points for each of the questions in parts B and C

LESSON 14
Ezra Helps His People

I. Preparing to Read

Pointer Questions

1. What did Ezra teach?
2. What law did Artaxerxes make to the treasurers beyond the river?

II. Reader

* "How long had it taken to build the temple? [80 – 60 = 20 years]

* "Why were only those who desired to go to Jerusalem supposed to go? [Someone not interested would not be of much benefit.] What were the people to take along to Jerusalem?

* "Why was Ezra to use those who knew God's laws for teachers? [One cannot teach something well unless he knows it himself.]

"Whom did Ezra thank for the encouragement the letter gave him?"

** These questions should be discussed before asking the children to do part D of the workbook lesson.*

III. Workbook

ANSWER KEY

A. 1. They were sent to *find out how things were going* at Jerusalem.
2. a. the king
   b. counselors
   c. the people
   d. the priests
3. bullocks, rams, and lambs
4. They were to get these things *to offer on the altar.*
5. They were to do with it *whatever seemed good* to them.
6. They were to speedily *do whatever Ezra asked.*
7. pay taxes
8. a. death
   b. banishment
   c. taking away goods
   d. putting in prison

B. 1. diligently
2. freely
3. willingly
4. quickly
5. speedily
6. diligently
7. speedily
8. deeply

C. 1. b. teacher
2. governor
3. king
4. scribe
5. counselors
6. treasurers
7. a. singers
   b. porters
   c. ministers
8. a. officers
   b. judges

D. 1. twenty years
2. People who did not want to go would not be much help.
3. They could not teach the laws if they did not know them.

LESSON 15
Joy and Sorrow

I. Preparing to Read

Pointer Questions

1. What gave the people joy?
2. What brought sorrow?

II. Reader

"At what river did the people gather before they started for Jerusalem? See the map in Lesson 5 of the workbook. [Euphrates]

"Why did they not want the king's soldiers to go with them for protection? [They had told the king their God was able to protect them.]

"Had Ezra married someone from the land of Canaan? Why did he tell God he was ashamed? [It was his people who had done wrong, and that made him feel bad. He may also have felt some responsibility because he was a teacher and might have been able to help the people do better.]"

III. Workbook

ANSWER KEY

A.

3	8	12	16
5	6	15	18
2	7	13	20
4	10	14	19
1	9	11	17

B. 1. at the evening sacrifice
2. on his knees
3. O my God
4. ashamed
5. because of the sins
6. because of their sins
7. (Any of the following)
   He let a few escape.
   reviving in their slavery
   mercy in the sight of the kings of Persia
   reviving to repair the temple and the wall
8. the prophets
9. The land was an *unclean land.*
10. a. so they would *be strong*
    b. so they could *eat the good of the land*
    c. so they could *leave it to their children*
11. no

C. (Correction points underlined)

1. Ezra had been ashamed to ask the king for soldiers to help them fight the enemies along the way.
2. The Jews who were living in the land were disobeying God.
3. The people of Cannan caused the Jews to do evil things.
4. Ezra's joy was turned to sorrow.
5. He tore his clothes and pulled out the hair of his head.

LESSON 16
The People Repent

I. Preparing to Read

Pointer Questions

1. What did the people do about their sin?
2. Why would Ezra not eat or drink?

II. Reader

Test the children's comprehension with this oral quiz. Have them number a paper from 1–10 and write a word or phrase for the blank in each sentence you say.

1. Ezra prayed, confessed, and cried before the ____. (house of God / temple)
2. The people of Israel had taken strange ____ of the people of the land. (wives)
3. One of the men told ____ to get up and be responsible to see that the matter was taken care of. (Ezra)
4. Ezra would not eat or drink because of the ____ of the people. (sins)
5. An announcement was made, telling all the people to gather at ____. (Jerusalem)
6. They were to gather together within ____ days. (three)
7. All the people came and sat in the ____. (street)
8. They trembled because of their sin and because of the ____. (rain)
9. The men promised to ____ their strange wives and the children born to them. (put away)
10. In about two ____ everything was settled. (months)

Discussion

"Was the gathering at Jerusalem a joyful one?

"Were the people willing to do what Ezra said they should? Why was it not done right away?"

III. Workbook

ANSWER KEY

A. 1

B. 4, 10, 1
8, 6, 2
3, 7, 5

C. (Individual work)

D. 1. c
2. b
3. a
4. b

LESSON 17
Nehemiah's Request

I. Preparing to Read

Pointer Questions

1. How did Nehemiah find out about things at Jerusalem?
2. Why did the Jews love Jerusalem?

II. Reader

"How long did Nehemiah pray? For what did he pray?

"What plans did Nehemiah make before he left for Jerusalem? [He asked for letters to secure safe traveling and timber.]"

III. Workbook

ANSWER KEY

A.
1. thirteen, Persia
2. eager
3. in great trouble and disgrace
4. broken, burned
5. Shushan
6. drinks
7. attentive, open
8. terribly, Moses
9. the king
10. months
11. sick
12. sorrow of heart
13. what he would request
14. prayed to God
15. send him
16. the queen, sitting

B.
I. A. Jew
B. Shushan
C. the king his drinks
D. king's cupbearer
E. his Jewish brethren

II. A. trouble and disgrace
B. broken down
C. burned with fire

III. A. the God of heaven
B. the children of Israel
C. what He said to Moses
D. His servant and the servants who want to fear His Name
E. find mercy in the sight of the king

C. 1. d
2. c
3. g
4. a
5. b
6. f
7. e
8. h

D. 1. porters
2. appeased
3. cupbearer
4. blush
5. scepter
6. provinces
7. Purim
8. gallows
9. banquet
10. perplexed
11. boasted
12. reviving
13. banishment
14. distressing
15. diligently
16. perish

LESSON 18
Nehemiah Goes to Jerusalem

I. Preparing to Read

Pointer Questions

1. How did Nehemiah find out just what the conditions were at Jerusalem?
2. What did the Jews say when Nehemiah told them his plans?

II. Reader

It would be ideal to have a sketch of the city wall and the brook on the blackboard. (See the map in the workbook.) Trace Nehemiah's night journey in class from the Valley Gate to the Dung Gate, Fountain Gate, and King's Pool. Then follow the brook north. We do not know how far he went before he turned around, perhaps the whole way to the northeast corner.

"Why do you think Nehemiah went in the night to look at the wall? [He probably did not want everyone to know what he had in mind.] Who did not like it when they found out why Nehemiah was there?"

III. Workbook

When correcting the workbook, you may want to have the children give the information for the questions answered *yes* in part A.

ANSWER KEY

A. 1. no
2. no
3. yes (at night)
4. no
5. yes (the gate of the valley)
6. no
7. yes (after seeing the wall)
8. yes (to remove the disgrace)
9. yes (Nehemiah's urging)
10. yes (grieved)
11. yes (laughed at the Jews)
12. yes (God will prosper)
13. no
14. yes (all of it)
15. no

B. These places marked with *X*:
Valley Gate
Fountain Gate
King's Pool
Brook Kidron

C. c

D. 1. b
2. a
3. a
4. b
5. b
6. b
7. b
8. b
9. b
10. a

E. "Let us get up and build."

F. 1. Mordecai, Esther
2. Artaxerxes, Ezra
3. A man of Judah, Ezra
4. Nehemiah, the Jews

LESSON 19
Enemies Try to Hinder the Work

I. Preparing to Read

Pointer Questions

1. Why were the heaps of rubbish a bad thing?
2. What were the people to do if they heard the trumpet?

II. Reader

"For what could the Jews use the stones out of the heaps of the rubbish which were burned?

"What is a good thing to do when people laugh at us and despise us? [Pray to God. Go on with our work.]

"What makes work go well and fast? [workers that have a mind to work; God's blessing]"

III. Workbook

ANSWER KEY

A. 1. the Jews
2. Sanballat
3. Tobiah
4. Sanballat
5. Nehemiah
6. burden bearers
7. Jews who lived among the enemies
8. Nehemiah
9. the enemies
10. God

B. 1. the wall
2. making fun
3. a fox
4. a. prayed
b. kept on working
5. rubbish
6. weapons

C. 1. when
2. where
3. when
4. why
5. where
6. when
7. why
8. where
9. where
10. why
11. when
12. where
13. where
14. where
15. when
16. why

D. 1. a. The enemies *made fun* of the Jews
   b. They *decided to fight* against the Jews.
2. a. Nehemiah *prayed* to God.
   b. He *kept on working.*
3. The people had *a mind to work.*
4. a. They *prayed* to their God.
   b. They *set men to watch* for the enemy day and night.
5. He encouraged them not to *be afraid.*
6. a. He encouraged them to *remember their great God.*
   b. He encouraged them to *fight* to save their families and houses.

Gradebook: 53 points, counting two for each sentence answer

LESSON 20
Trouble in Judah

I. Preparing to Read

Pointer Questions

1. Why did some of the poor people sell their lands and houses?
2. What did the rich Jews have to give back to the poor brethren?

II. Reader

"What kind of testimony were the rich Jews giving to the enemies? [Their actions were telling people that they were selfish and unkind.] What kind of testimony should they have been giving? [Their lives should have shown that God's people are loving and fair.]

"How was Nehemiah a good example?

"What is a person's lap? How could Nehemiah shake out his lap? [He shook the part of his robe that would be on his lap while sitting. Nothing could stay on his lap that way, and he wanted it to be a sign of how every man who did not keep his promise would be cast away.]"

III. Workbook

ANSWER KEY

A.
1. P
2. P
3. R
4. R
5. P
6. N
7. N
8. N
9. R
10. R
11. N
12. N

B.
1. c
2. a
3. c
4. b
5. b
6. c
7. c
8. a
9. a
10. c
11. a
12. b

C. 1. The *rich were not treating their poorer brethren fairly.*
2. (Any four)
Some people had to *sell their lands and houses.*
Some had to *mortgage their lands or borrow money.*
Some *daughters had to go for slaves.*
Some of their *sons were in danger of becoming slaves.*
The poor were *crying out* against the rich.
3. They were *not treating one another fairly.*
4. (Any three)
He *did not ask them to do anything he would not do.*
He *had not been unfair* to them.
He *did not expect them to feed him.*
He *worked* with the people in building the wall.

LESSON 21
The Enemy Tries Again

I. Preparing to Read

Pointer Questions

1. What did Sanballat say was the reason the Jews were building the wall?
2. How many times did the enemies ask Nehemiah to meet with them?

II. Reader

"Why could the enemies not get any of their schemes to work? [God was helping Nehemiah and the Jews.]

"What work was Nehemiah doing when the enemies asked him to come meet with them? [setting up the gates]"

III. Workbook

ANSWER KEY

A. 1. wall
2. gates
3. act friendly
4. village in the plain of Ono
5. do mischief
6. he was doing a great work
7. Five
8. scare
9. true
10. be Judah's king
11. sin
12. pray to his God
13. strengthen him
14. easily

B. (First word here crossed out in sentence)
1. herd, heard
2. there, their
3. maid, made
4. two, to

5. wood, would
6. too, to
7. weigh, way
8. cent, sent
9. meat, meet
10. plane, plain
11. new, knew
12. grate, great
13. eye, I
14. for, four
15. knot, not

C. 2
5
1
4
3

D. 1. salvation
2. faith
3. the Spirit
4. truth
5. righteousness
6. peace

LESSON 22
Ezra Teaches the People

I. Preparing to Read

Pointer Questions

1. Why were the enemies discouraged?
2. What directions did Nehemiah give the two rulers?

II. Reader

"What work was there to be done after the walls and gates were finished? [houses to build, ruling and direction of the work, watchman duty to protect the people]

"Other activities were taking place besides the building work. What did the people do in regards to their family history? [tried to find out from which family they came]

"What did they do in regards to God's Law? [gathered in the street at the water gate to hear Ezra read]"

III. Workbook

Practice for part D by wording a question and having the class compose multiple answer choices.

ANSWER KEY

A. 1. days
2. discouraged
3. good
4. frighten
5. two
6. the sun was hot
7. God
8. a few
9. Jews
10. not allowed
11. servants than singers
12. horses than mules
13. donkeys than mules
14. donkeys than camels
15. in the street in front of the water gate
16. Ezra
17. morning until noon
18. stood up

B.
1. yes (All their efforts to hinder the Jews failed.)
2. yes (The nobles seemed to think he was quite a good man.)
3. no (He tried to make Nehemiah afraid. He was with the enemies.)
4. no (Tobiah's response to Nehemiah's words was an attempt to make him afraid.)
5. yes (He gave direction for control of the gates and for watchmen to guard the city.)
6. yes (The walls would help protect them as they built their houses.)
7. yes (God put that desire in Nehemiah's heart.)
8. yes (42,360 + 7,337 + 245 = 49,942)
9. no (736 + 245 + 735 + 6,720 = 8,436)
10. yes (Everyone listened carefully.)
11. no (He was standing on the pulpit.)
12. yes (They stood up when Ezra opened it.)

C. (Drawing should include these items)
Ezra on a pulpit
many people below
six men on *Ezra's* right
seven men on *Ezra's* left
book in Ezra's hand

D. (Individual work)

LESSON 23
The People Obey the Law

I. Preparing to Read

Pointer Questions

1. From what did the people make their booths?
2. What did the people do when the booths were finished?

II. Reader

"Why do you think the people wept when they heard the reading? [They probably realized from the Law that they had not obeyed God's commandments.]

"Why were the people glad for eight days? Why were they sad on the ninth day?

"About whom did the Levites speak first in their prayer? [They spoke of God and His greatness.]"

III. Workbook

Discuss some of the answers for part C. Note the *and's* where the reader answers question 2. The children should separate the details to write their list of answers. Where the reader answers question 4, point out the semicolons as dividers between the answers. Explain question 5.

ANSWER KEY

A.
1. g
2. f
3. a
4. b
5. d
6. h
7. c
8. e

B.
1. the Feast of Tabernacles
2. every year
3. the seventh month
4. seven days
5. booths
6. a happy time
7. at the end of harvest time
8. read in the Book of the Law

C.
1. They had a *solemn meeting.*
2. (Any six of these)
   They *gathered together.*
   They *fasted.*
   They *put on sackcloth.*
   They *put earth on themselves.*
   They *separated themselves* form strangers.
   They *confessed their sins.*
   They *confessed the sins of their fathers.*
   They *heard the Book of the Law.*
   They *worshiped* the Lord.
3. "Blessed be Your glorious Name, which is higher than all blessing and praise."
4. a. God made heaven, the heaven of *heavens, with all their host.*
   b. God made the *earth, and all things that are in it.*
   c. God made the *seas, and all that is in them.*
5. (No answer expected)

D.
1. b
2. c
3. c
4. a
5. b
6. b
7. a
8. c
9. a
10. b

LESSON 24
The Prayer Continued

I. Preparing to Read

Pointer Questions

1. What did God do when His people were hungry and thirsty?
2. What did God's people do to the prophets?

II. Reader

Test reading comprehension with this oral quiz. Have the children number their papers from 1–15 and write *true* or *false* for each statement.

1. God showed mercy on Pharaoh and his servants. (false)
2. God divided the desert in front of His people. (false)
3. He led the Israelites during the day by a pillar of fire. (false)
4. God gave His laws from the Mount of Olives. (false)
5. God sent bread from heaven to feed His people. (true)
6. The children of Israel obeyed the laws God gave. (false)
7. They appointed a captain to take them back to Egypt. (true)

8. They made a molten lamb and called it their god. (false)
9. God kept His people supplied in the wilderness eighty years. (false)
10. God made new clothes for them while they traveled. (false)
11. God brought the children of Israel into the land He had promised their fathers. (true)
12. The children of Israel killed the prophets that told them of their sin. (true)
13. God let their enemies overcome them when Israel sinned. (true)
14. God delivered His people when they cried to Him in trouble. (true)
15. When Israel sinned again, God destroyed them altogether. (false)

Discussion

"How did the people throw the Law behind their backs? [They despised it and disobeyed it.]

"Do you know who were some of the saviors God sent to save His people from their enemies? [Samson, Ehud, Gideon, and other judges from many years before]"

III. Workbook

ANSWER KEY

A. (Individual work)

B. 1. of great kindness
long-suffering
slow to anger
generous
gracious
loving
merciful

2. provoking
stubborn
murderous
proud
disobedient
unthankful
rebellious

C. (Accept reasonable variations.)

1. a. slow to anger
b. merciful
c. long-suffering
d. generous

2. a. rebellious
b. unthankful
c. provoking
d. murderous

D. (First word here to be crossed out in sentence)

1. pillow, pillar
2. hungry, hunger
3. bought, brought
4. angry, anger
5. bandage, bondage
6. commended, commanded
7. moldy, molten
8. chickens, children
9. cloths, clothes
10. smell, swell

LESSON 25
The People's Promises

I. Preparing to Read

Pointer Questions

1. Who signed the promises that were written?
2. What noise was heard a long way off from Jerusalem?

II. Reader

"Did the Levites think the people deserved all the trouble that God had brought upon them?

"Who was getting rich from the good land God had given His people? [The kings who were ruling over them.]

"What did the people promise?"

III. Workbook

Let the children practice reading the phrases in part B orally, putting a distinct pause at the end of each line. It may help them to realize that a meaningful phrase often ends with a noun or verb.

Do a few numbers in part C together, discussing relationships between the words. Words that relate are not necessarily synonyms, nor do they all relate in the same way.

ANSWER KEY

A. (Any eight of these)

They promised to *keep all the commandments* of God.

They promised *not to let their sons or daughters marry people of the land.*

They promised *not to buy things on the Sabbath Day* or on a holy day.

They promised *not to plant crops every seventh year.*

They promised *not to harvest what came up of itself* in the seventh year.

They promised *to forgive debts* in the seventh year.

They promised *to bring their first ripe fruit* to the Lord.

They promised *to bring their first-born sons* to the house of the Lord.

They promised *to bring their first-born animals* to the house of the Lord.

They promised *to give the Lord one-tenth* of all that they received.

B.
1. a
2. b
3. a
4. b
5. a
6. b
7. b
8. a
9. b

C.
1. queen, scepter, Mordecai
2. rebellious, wicked, proud
3. joy, booths, seven
4. governor, cupbearer, prayer
5. scribe, teacher, pulpit
6. wicked, proud, gallows, letters
7. tricks, enemy, mean

8. kind, merciful, great, mighty, commandments
9. king, Vashti, Esther, scepter
10. palace, banquet, king

D.
1. wall
2. Sabbath
3. dedication
4. poor

LESSON 26
More Work to Do

I. Preparing to Read

Pointer Questions

1. Where was Nehemiah when Tobiah got a room in the temple?
2. Why were the Levites not doing the work in the house of the Lord?

II. Reader

"What promises that the people made in Lesson 25 were they not keeping? [to give one-tenth of all they got to the Lord, to not buy on the Sabbath, to not marry Moabites or Ammonites]

"What were the Levites supposed to have for their living?"

III. Workbook

In part A, the paragraph numbers tell where to find the account of the sin. Nehemiah's response to each situation may be found in other paragraphs.

ANSWER KEY

A.
1. a. One of the high priests joined himself to Tobiah and gave him a room in the temple.
   b. Nehemiah threw Tobiah's things out of the room, commanded it to be cleaned, and then brought in the temple vessels.
2. a. The Levites were not doing their work in the temple, and they were not getting what belonged to them.
   b. Nehemiah set the Levites in their place in the temple and had the people bring in their tithes.
3. a. People were working and buying things on the Sabbath day.
   b. Nehemiah scolded the people and commanded that the gates of Jerusalem be shut for the Sabbath.
4. a. Some of the Jews had married women of Moab and Ammon.
   b. Nehemiah scolded them, cursed them, hit some of them, and pulled out their hair. He made them promise not to let their children marry Moabites or Ammonites.

B.
1. Vashti
2. Ezra
3. Cyrus
4. Belshazzar
5. Artaxerxes
6. Mordecai
7. Ezekiel
8. Daniel
9. Nehemiah
10. Esther
11. Tobiah
12. Darius
13. Noadiah

C.
1. b
2. b
3. a
4. c
5. a
6. c
7. b
8. c
9. b
10. b
11. a
12. b
13. a
14. b
15. c
16. b
17. b
18. c

Gradebook: 47 points, counting two points for each answer in part A

LESSON 27
The Story of Jonah—Part 1

I. Preparing to Read

Pointer Questions

1. Why was there a great storm on the sea?
2. How did the sailors find out who was to blame for the storm?

II. Reader

"Why would Jonah not want to preach that Nineveh would be destroyed if God did not destroy it all? [That would make him look like a false prophet.] Would the people think he was a false prophet? [No, if they repented and were saved, it was because they believed him.]

"What did the men mean when they said, 'Do not let us die for this man's life'? [They were afraid if they kept Jonah on board to save his life, they would all die in the storm.] What did they mean when they said, 'Do not hold us guilty of killing an innocent man'? [They were afraid if they threw Jonah overboard to stop the storm, he might be innocent after all and they would be guilty of his death.]"

III. Workbook

ANSWER KEY

A.
4
2
7
3
1
5
6

B.
1. great
2. heathen
3. opposite
4. great
5. mighty
6. tempestuous / great
7. dry
8. great
9. raging
10. innocent
11. Jonah's / great
12. great

C. Circle numbers 1, 3, 5, 7, 8, 10, 12. Cross out sentences 2, 4, 6, 9, 11.

D. (Individual work)

E. 1. a. important
b. favorite
c. large
d. mighty
2. a. teach
b. explain
c. advise
d. preach
3. a. burn
b. break
c. throw away
d. kill
4. a. beat
b. pull
c. switch
d. spank

LESSON 28
The Story of Jonah—Part 2

I. Preparing to Read

Pointer Questions

1. What made it uncomfortable in the belly of the fish?
2. What law did the king of Nineveh make?

II. Reader

"What do you think the promises could have been that Jonah said he would keep? [Perhaps as a prophet Jonah had promised to serve and obey God. Such a promise would have been broken when he tried to run away.]

"Who was pleased about the change in Nineveh? Who was displeased?

"Was Jonah sorry to see a gourd destroyed? Would he have been sorry to see a great city destroyed?

"What kind of people cannot tell the difference between their right hand or left hand? [Little children who would have been innocent of the wickedness of Nineveh. They would have been destroyed too if God destroyed the city.]"

III. Workbook

In preparation for part E, summarize the story with the class. List six or eight main events to give the children an idea what to draw. Then have them draw lines to make blocks for their pictures.

ANSWER KEY

A. 1. a great fish
2. no
3. three days and three nights
4. God
5. vomited
6. three days
7. forty
8. yes
9. no
10. no

B. 1. a great fish
2. a gourd
3. a worm
4. a hot east wind

C. 1. gracious
2. merciful
3. slow to anger
4. of great kindness

D. 1. Jonah, Joppa
2. fare, Tarshish
3. asleep, wind
4. afraid, prayed
5. master, die
6. sea, calm
7. way
8. Lord
9. fish, pray
10. go, preach
11. believed

E. (Individual work)

LESSON 29
The Books of the Old Testament

I. Preparing to Read

Pointer Questions

1. What books did Solomon write?
2. Which prophets told things about Jesus?

II. Reader

"Which prophet besides Jonah gave warning to Nineveh? About how many years after Jonah's preaching was Nineveh destroyed? [50 + 20 = 70 years]

"When did the prophets Haggai and Zechariah live? [at the time of the Persian king Darius when the Jews renewed the building of the temple which had been stopped—Lesson 7] When Haggai said, 'Consider your ways,' he wanted the people to think how wrong it was for them to be paying attention only to their own houses when God's house was unfinished."

III. Workbook

Give some direction for the writing in part D. Tell the children to write what the person was (king, queen, prophet . . .) without telling the name, and something the person did or something memorable he said.

Provide time later for the children to read their riddles.

ANSWER KEY

A. 1. d
2. e
3. a
4. b
5. c
6. h
7. j
8. g
9. i
10. f

B. 1. most of
2. 17
3. the prophets said would happen
4. 150
5. 400
6. John the Baptist

C. *Across*
2. interesting
3. Solomon
11. Zephaniah
12. herdsman
13. Habakkuk

15. Proverbs
17. Joel
19. Lamentations
20. will
23. Zechariah
26. after
27. one
28. Obadiah
29. Daniel
30. worms

Down
1. Hosea
2. in
4. Micah
5. John
6. Lord
7. Ezekiel
8. Haggai
9. Malachi
10. Job
14. great
15. Psalms
16. Isaiah
17. Jonah
18. Jeremiah
21. Spirit
22. David
24. Amos
25. Nahum
27. Old

D. (Individual work)

LESSON 30
Beautiful Writings From the Old Testament

I. Preparing to Read

Pointer Questions

1. What reason to rejoice is there in Habakkuk 3:17, 18?
2. Why would a book of remembrance be written?

II. Reader

"What could one taste to see that the Lord is good? [To take a taste of something means to try it, not necessarily putting it in the mouth. David meant that people should not be afraid to come to the Lord and see what His Word says, and let Him direct their lives. They would find out by experience that God is good.]

"What is the meaning of Micah 5:2?"

III. Workbook

Recommend that the children use the table of contents if they need help for part B. They should find a story by the title and skim it for the information that would answer their question.

ANSWER KEY

A.
1. keep
2. redeemer, earth
3. sleep, safety
4. child, right
5. Remember, evil
6. praise, ashamed
7. name, earth
8. good, trouble, trust
9. book, feared
10. word, heart, sin
11. gold
12. good

B.
1. g
2. c
3. a
4. f
5. h
6. e
7. d
8. b
9. o
10. p
11. j
12. i
13. k
14. m
15. n
16. l

C. 1. f
2. h
3. b
4. a
5. c
6. e
7. d
8. j
9. g
10. i

D. (Possible answers)
1. listen
2. the face
3. acted or behaved
4. made known openly
5. twisted around
6. business, trade, or work
7. wildly stormy
8. a load of goods

TEST

ANSWER KEY

A. 1. m
2. h
3. e
4. k
5. i
6. n
7. d
8. a
9. f
10. c
11. j
12. b
13. l
14. g

B. 1. tongue
2. Daniel
3. Cedar
4. fox
5. gallows
6. changed
7. fasted
8. letter
9. wives
10. sad
11. wall
12. poor
13. Tabernacles
14. booths
15. Tarshish
16. Proverbs

C. 1. affliction
2. visions
3. perplexed
4. terrified
5. boasted
6. distinctly
7. scepter
8. pulpit
9. cargo
10. perish
11. orphan
12. possess

D. Isaiah
Jeremiah
Ezekiel
Daniel
Hosea
Joel
Amos
Obadiah
Jonah
Micah
Nahum
Habakkuk
Zephaniah
Haggai
Zechariah
Malachi

Gradebook: 58 test points

Unit Five

Stories About Jesus From the Gospel of Luke

UNIT 5
General Plan

The lessons in Unit 5 follow the pattern established in previous units.

Continue to promote independence in the workbook lessons. Have the children do all they can by memory before referring to the reader for answers.

Remember to remove the unit tests before distributing the workbooks.

Unit 5 Lessons

Lesson **Page**

LESSON 1
The Birth of John Is Announced

I. Preparing to Read

Pointer Questions

1. What does *Gospel* mean?
2. What was done at the hours of prayer?

II. Reader

"To what tribe of Israel did Zacharias belong? [the tribe of Levi, because only Levites were priests]"

In discussing the priests' work, refer to the temple diagram in the reader. For a large class, you may want to sketch the diagram on the board.

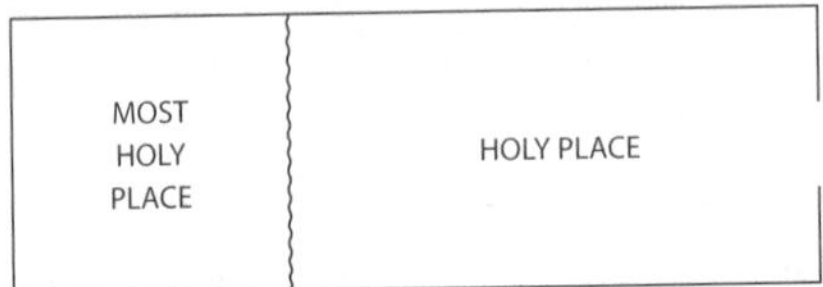

Indicate on the diagram where Zacharias was when the angel talked to him.

III. Workbook

ANSWER KEY

A. 1. a. They *saw* the things He did.
   b. They *heard* the things He said.
   c. *Others told them* about Jesus.
2. *Luke* wrote these stories.
3. He wrote so that *others would know the things they heard were true.*
4. The stories are about *Jesus.*
5. We know these stories are true because *what Luke wrote is the Word of God.*
6. (Any order)
   a. The *ashes* at the altar were *cleaned away.*
   b. More *wood was put on the fire.*
   c. The *lamps* of the candlestick were *trimmed.*
   d. The *altar* of incense was *cleaned.*
   e. *Fresh bread* was put on the table.
7. The *priests* did this work.
8. The work was started *before it was sunlight.*
9. a. They *offered a lamb.*
   b. They *burned incense.*
10. The people *worshiped* outside the holy place.
11. These were the *hours of prayer.*
12. Zacharias was in the holy place, and the *others were outside.*
13. The angel's name was *Gabriel.*

14. (Any order)
    a. His *name shall be John.*
    b. He *shall not drink wine* or strong drink.
    c. He *shall be filled with God's Spirit.*
    d. He *shall help many people* in Israel to repent.

B. 1. Levi
2. Matthew, Mark, John

C. (Numbers will be marked according to individual knowledge. Correct answers are given for your convenience in class discussion.)
1. Gabriel
2. Mary
3. They were cousins.
4. Bethlehem
5. Caesar Augustus
6. in the temple
7. The Spirit came and sat upon Him like a dove.
8. all night
9. Simon, Andrew, James, John, Philip, Thomas, Matthew, James, Simon, Judas, Judas, Batholomew

Simon	Matthew
Andrew	James
James	Simon
John	Judas
Philip	Judas
Thomas	Batholomew

10. a sinful woman
11. healing on the Sabbath
    not washing before eating
    saying He was God's Son
    eating with sinners
12. the Pharisees
13. Judas Iscariot
14. Pilate
15. Calvary
16. "Father, forgive them, for they do not know what they do."
17. Joseph of Arimathaea
18. Bethany

LESSON 2
The Birth of Jesus Is Announced

I. Preparing to Read

Pointer Questions

1. Why did Zacharias and Elisabeth name their son John?
2. How did Zacharias show what he wanted the child's name to be?

II. Reader

"How did Elisabeth know that Mary would be the mother of the Lord? [She was filled with the Holy Ghost. She knew it by God's Spirit.]

"Where did Mary go after the angel talked with her?" On a map, point out the distance from Nazareth to the hill country of Judea, a trip of approximately seventy miles.

III. Workbook

ANSWER KEY

A.
1. Mary
2. Elisabeth
3. Mary
4. Mary
5. Mary
6. Elisabeth
7. Elisabeth
8. Elisabeth
9. Mary
10. Elisabeth
11. Elisabeth
12. Mary
13. Mary
14. Elisabeth
15. Mary
16. Mary
17. Elisabeth

B.
1. Nazareth
2. Galilee
3. Judea
4. Jerusalem

C.
1. Daniel d
2. Abraham e
3. Joseph a
4. Mordecai b
5. Jesus c
6. Elijah f
7. Moses j
8. Ruth g
9. David i
10. Jeremiah h

D.
1. d
2. f
3. h
4. e
5. b
6. c
7. a
8. j
9. i
10. g

LESSON 3
Jesus Is Born

I. Preparing to Read

Pointer Questions

1. Why did Jesus have a manger bed?
2. Who was at the temple when Jesus was taken there?

II. Reader

Give an oral quiz in place of part or all of the discussion. Have the children write *yes* or *no* for each number as you ask the questions below.

1. Was the world ruled by Caesar Augustus? (yes)
2. Did the high priest decide that everyone should be taxed? (no)
3. Did Joseph and Mary live in Jerusalem? (no)
4. Were Joseph and Mary of David's family line? (yes)
5. Did Joseph and Mary go to Bethlehem to offer a sacrifice? (no)
6. Could Joseph and Mary get to Bethlehem in one day? (no)
7. Was Jesus born at Bethlehem? (yes)
8. Did Joseph and Mary stay at the inn? (no)
9. Were the shepherds in the country of Galilee? (no)

10. Was the news of the Saviour brought to them by an angel? (yes)
11. Did more than one angel appear to the shepherds? (yes)
12. Did the shepherds go to find Jesus right away? (yes)
13. Did the shepherds tell anyone what they had heard? (yes)
14. Was Jesus named the same day He was born? (no)
15. Did Joseph and Mary take Jesus to the temple when He was eight days old? (no)
16. Did they offer a lamb for a sacrifice? (no)
17. Did Simeon come to Bethlehem to see Jesus? (no)
18. Did Simeon bless God when he saw the child Jesus? (yes)
19. Was Anna a widow? (yes)
20. Did Anna thank God when she came to Joseph and Mary? (yes)

III. Workbook

ANSWER KEY

A.

1. b	12. c		
2. c	13. c		
3. c	14. a		
4. a	15. c		
5. a	16. a		
6. c	17. b		
7. a	18. a		
8. a	19. c		
9. c	20. a		
10. c	21. b		
11. b	22. c		

B.
1. ***B*** ethlehem
2. ***A*** ugustus
3. ***B*** aby
4. ***Y*** ou
5. ***J*** udea
6. ***E*** arth
7. ***S*** hepherds
8. ***U*** s
9. ***S*** waddling

C.
1. glory
2. glorify
3. glorified
4. glorious

LESSON 4
The Early Life of Jesus and John

I. Preparing to Read

Pointer Questions

1. What was Jesus doing in the temple?
2. What did John require before he baptized people?

II. Reader

"What was Jesus' Father's business? [God's plan for Jesus to be the Saviour]

"Who was the One mightier than John who would come after him? What did John mean in his description by 'His fan is in His hand, and He will thoroughly clean His floor'? [He was comparing Jesus to a farmer on the threshing floor. The floor was a flat area where the grain stalks were trampled to break the kernels out of the chaff. The fan was an instrument used like a shovel to throw the threshed material up into the air. The breeze would blow the light chaff and straw to the side and the clean grain would fall straight down. This separation of good grain from the useless chaff was a description John the Baptist used to teach that Jesus would separate the righteous and wicked people.]"

III. Workbook

ANSWER KEY

A. (Possible answers; children should have four things listed.)
- Jesus was listening to the leaders.
- Jesus was asking questions.
- Jesus understood the Bible.
- Jesus wanted to obey His heavenly Father.
- Jesus wanted to obey His earthly parents.
- Jesus submitted to what His parents wanted.

B.
1. c
2. a
3. d
4. b

C.
1. b
2. c
3. a
4. e
5. d

D.
1. yes
2. yes
3. no
4. He baptized people.
5. yes
6. no
7. a. confess their sins
   b. stop doing wrong things
8. They thought they were good people.
9. raise up children to Abraham
10. trees

E.
1. tidings
2. Swaddling
3. humble
4. inn
5. handmaid
6. custom
7. stature
8. Hail
9. manger
10. decree
11. multitude
12. submitted

LESSON 5
Jesus Is Tempted

I. Preparing to Read

Pointer Questions

1. What was Jesus used to doing on the Sabbath Day?
2. Why did the people of Nazareth think that Jesus could not be anyone great?

II. Reader

"What does 'Man shall not live by bread alone' mean? [Food to keep the body alive is not the only thing to consider in life. Even more important is the spiritual matter of obedience to God."]

"Did Jesus mean Satan should not be tempting Him when He said, 'You shall not tempt the Lord your God'? [He meant it would be wrong for Him to throw Himself from the temple. To purposely do something dangerous apart from God's will is tempting God to let one become hurt.]

"What made the people angry at Jesus' words? [He was saying that other people would believe in Him and be helped, but they would not get help because they would not believe.]"

III. Workbook

ANSWER KEY

A.
1. b
2. e
3. a
4. c
5. d

B.
1. "It is written that man shall not live by bread alone, but by every word of God."
2. "Get behind Me, Satan, because it is written, 'You shall worship the Lord your God, and Him only shall you serve.'"
3. "It is said, 'You shall not tempt the Lord your God.'"

C.
1. c
2. f
3. e
4. a
5. d
6. b

D.
1. A *widow* in Sidon and the leper *Naaman* were blessed in the Old Testament.
2. Naaman *came to Elisha* to be healed.
3. The widow *took care of Elijah.*
4. a. They *would not care for Jesus.*
   b. They *would not come to Jesus* for help.
   (You may accept: They *would not believe* in Him.)
5. They tried to *throw Him over the brow of the hill* where their city was built.

E.
2. a. raindrops
   b. rain drops
3. a. in deed
   b. Indeed
4. a. rest less
   b. restless
5. a. around
   b. a round
6. a. black board
   b. blackboard
7. a. a loud
   b. aloud
8. a. sun rise
   b. sunrise
9. a. be long
   b. belong
10. a. forgiving
    b. for giving

11. a. below
    b. be low
12. a. A stray
    b. astray
13. a. homeless
    b. home less

Gradebook: 50 points, counting two points for each sentence in part D

LESSON 6
Jesus Teaches and Heals

I. Preparing to Read

Pointer Questions

1. What amazed the people?
2. When did the men usually do their fishing?

II. Reader

"How did the devils know that Jesus is the son of God? [Devils have Satan's power and know things of the spirit world that people do not have ability to see.]

"Why was the healed leper supposed to show himself to the priest? [In the Law of Moses (Leviticus 13; 14) directions were given for the priest to be in charge of inspection of the leper to determine if he was allowed to live among other people. A cleansed leper was to bring an offering.]"

III. Workbook

ANSWER KEY

A.
1. yes
2. yes
3. yes
4. no
5. yes
6. no
7. yes
8. yes
9. James, John
10. no
11. yes
12. yes
13. He was sent.
14. yes
15. men in sin
16. yes
17. yes
18. to pray

B.
1. Jesus *said* to the devil, "Keep still and come out of him."
2. Jesus *stood over her and rebuked the fever.*
3. He *laid his hands on them.*
4. Jesus *touched* the man *and said,* "I will. Be clean."
5. The people were *amazed.*
6. Peter was *astonished.*
7. Everyone was *surprised.*

C.
1. Jesus of Nazareth
2. the Holy One of God
3. Christ
4. the Son of God

D.
1. c
2. c
3. c
4. b
5. c
6. b
7. a
8. a

LESSON 7
People Find Fault With Jesus

I. Preparing to Read

Pointer Questions

1. How did the man with palsy get into the house?
2. How did he get out of the house?
3. Why could Jesus not help the Pharisees?

II. Reader

"Could anyone but God forgive a man's sins? Could anyone but God heal a man by saying, 'Rise up and walk'? Is one thing easier than the other? [Neither could be done without the power of God. The fact that Jesus' words "Rise up and walk" were effective proved that He also had the right to say, "Your sins are forgiven."]

"How were the disciples of John the Baptist different from the disciples of Jesus? [John's disciples fasted.]"

III. Workbook

ANSWER KEY

A.
1. There were so *many people* in the house they could not get to Jesus.
2. They *did not know He is God's Son.*
3. The *publicans were often dishonest* and charged extra money to make themselves rich.
4. They only *pretended to keep the Law* and did not do things to please God.
5. The Pharisees fasted and prayed *to be seen of men.*
6. *Jesus came to help sinners.*

B.

1. F	11. F
2.	12.
3.	13.
4. F	14. F
5.	15. F
6. F	16.
7. F	17. F
8. F	18.
9.	19.
10. F	

C.

1. b	6. b
2. a	7. a
3. c	8. b
4. c	9. c
5. a	10. c

LESSON 8
Great Teachings of Jesus

I. Preparing to Read

Pointer Questions

1. Who were the twelve apostles?
2. Why was God not pleased with the giving of the scribes and Pharisees?

II. Reader

"What day of the week was the Sabbath Day? [Saturday]

"Where could the Pharisees have read what David did? [in the Old Testament]

"When had there been false prophets who lied to the people and the people spoke well of them? [In Ahab's day lying prophets told him he would be successful in battle. In Jeremiah's day lying prophets told the Jews all would be well if they did not yield to the Chaldeans. The people were pleased to hear these false promises.]"

III. Workbook

Review and drill the names of the twelve apostles. The students need not write the names in part B from memory, but keep reviewing daily until they have memorized the list.

This arrangement sung to the tune of "Bringing In the Sheaves" without the chorus may be a memory aid:

There were twelve disciples Jesus called to help Him;
Simon Peter, Andrew, James, his brother John,
Philip, Thomas, Matthew, James the son of Alphaeus,
Simon, Thaddaeus, Judas, and Bartholomew.
(Thaddaeus is another name for the Judas who was not Iscariot.)

ANSWER KEY

A.
1. e
2. h
3. b
4. c
5. d
6. a
7. g
8. i
9. f
10. j
11. k

B.
Simon
Andrew
James
John
Philip
Bartholomew
Matthew
Thomas
James
Simon
Judas
Judas

C.
1. No, the story tells about *different Sabbath days* and the choosing of the disciples *after a night* of prayer.
2. No, when the withered hand was healed, it was *like the other hand.*
3. No, they *asked one another how they could* do it.
4. No, He *prayed all that night.*
5. Yes, He chose the *twelve apostles from His disciples.*

D. 1. righteous, did what was right
2. old, well stricken in years
3. fear fell upon him, he was afraid
4. dumb, not able to speak
5. saluted, greeted
6. kin, relatives
7. marveled, wondered
8. kept . . . in her heart, did not tell
9. descended, came down
10. left, departed from
11. setting, going down

E. 1. Hannah
2. Anna
3. Mary
4. Shepherds
5. The Shunammite
6. Ezra
7. Nehemiah
8. A captive maid
9. Daniel
10. Mordecai
11. Boaz
12. An Israelite

Gradebook: 56 points, counting two points for each question in part C and one for each number in D.

LESSON 9
More Great Teachings of Jesus

I. Preparing to Read

Pointer Questions

1. When do sinners do good to others?
2. What is the Golden Rule?

II. Reader

"How can it be known what kind a tree is? What lesson did Jesus teach with this fact? [It can be known what kind of person someone is by the fruit that he brings forth, or the deeds that he does.]

"What must be done before a man can be a help to someone else? [He must realize his own need and let God help him.]"

III. Workbook

Review the names of the twelve apostles.

ANSWER KEY

A. 1. enemies
2. good
3. Bless; pray
4. hit your other cheek, too
5. your other coat, too
6. give it to him
7. ask him for it again
8. you want them to treat you
9. sinners
10. they think they will receive as much again
11. to receive anything back
12. be judged
13. be forgiven

B. 1. (Picture of a tree with good fruit)

2. (Picture of a tree with bad fruit)
3. (Picture of a house on the rock)
4. (Picture of a house falling in storm)

C. *Group one*

1. g	6. a
2. h	7. j
3. i	8. e
4. b	9. d
5. c	10. f

Group two

1. b	6. a
2. i	7. j
3. f	8. e
4. h	9. g
5. d	10. c

Group three

1. f	6. i
2. e	7. d
3. g	8. c
4. j	9. b
5. a	10. h

Group four

(Accept reasonable variations.)

1. g	6. b
2. j (a, b)	7. c
3. i (g)	8. h (j)
4. f (e)	9. d
5. a	10. e (a, d)

LESSON 10
Jesus Heals the Ruler's Servant

I. Preparing to Read

Pointer Questions

1. What had the Roman ruler done for the Jewish people?
2. What made the people say, "God has visited His people"?

II. Reader

"Why did the ruler explain to Jesus about the men under his authority? [He was telling Jesus that he understood authority, and he believed that a simple command from Jesus would heal his servant.]

"Why should the Pharisees have been quicker than a Roman to believe in Jesus? [The Pharisees studied the Scriptures, which had many prophecies about Jesus.]"

III. Workbook

Drill the names of the apostles.

ANSWER KEY

A.

1. c	5. b	9. b	13. a
2. b	6. c	10. b	14. b
3. a	7. a	11. c	15. a
4. a	8. c	12. b	16. c

B.
1. a shout of welcome or greeting
2. lowly in feeling; not proud
3. a woman servant
4. the usual way of doing it; habit
5. declared them guilty and worthy of punishment
6. an order or command
7. a place where travelers can get meals and a place to sleep
8. strips of cloth wrapped around the body
9. yielded; gave up to Him
10. news
11. size; height
12. power to make others obey
13. push out or set afloat
14. made a sign with the hand
15. tiles
16. a piece of furniture or mat on which to sleep or relax
17. tax collectors
18. greedy; eating too much

C.
1. finished
2. teaching
3. Roman
4. ruler
5. Jewish
6. begged
7. worthy
8. greatness
9. servants
10. turned
11. carried
12. sorrowing
13. pitied
14. greatly
15. messenger(s)
16. written
17. sitting
18. piped
19. drinking
20. gluttonous

D.
1. c
2. e
3. a
4. b
5. d

E. "Finally, brethren, whatsoever things are true, whatsoever things are honest, whatsoever things are just, whatsoever things are pure, whatsoever things are lovely, whatsoever things are of good report; if there be any virtue, and if there be any praise, think on these things."

LESSON 11
Jesus Visits in Simon's House

I. Preparing to Read

Pointer Questions

1. Why did Simon think Jesus would know the woman was a sinner?
2. What saved the woman from her sins?

II. Reader

Give an oral quiz, having the children write the name or identification of each character described.

1. The Pharisee who invited Jesus to his house (Simon)
2. The person who had His feet washed with tears (Jesus)
3. The one who knew what others were thinking (Jesus)
4. The one who told a story about two men who owed money (Jesus)
5. The one who had greater love for the man who forgave them (the man who owed most)
6. The one who kissed Jesus' feet (the woman)
7. The one to whom Jesus said, "Your sins are forgiven." (the woman)
8. The one who did not see how sinful he was (Simon)
9. Those who were with Jesus as He went preaching to every city and village (the twelve apostles)
10. Some women who gave of their own things to supply Jesus' needs (Joanna, Susanna, Mary Magdalene)
11. The one out of whom Jesus cast seven devils (Mary Magdalene)
12. The ones who were not supposed to understand Jesus' parables (those who would not believe and obey)
13. The one who takes away the Word so people will not believe (the devil)
14. The ones who stood outside, wanting to see Jesus (His mother and brothers)
15. The people who are Jesus' mother and brothers (those who hear and obey God's Word)

III. Workbook

A short cut for part D would be to allow the children to number the sentences in the answer list and then put those numbers at the appropriate places on the outline.

ANSWER KEY

A.
1. T
2. F
3. T
4. F
5. T
6. F
7. F
8. F
9. T
10. T
11. F
12. F
13. F
14. F
15. F
16. T
17. F
18. F
19. F
20. F

B. *Across*
2. wiped
6. peace
7. woman
8. little
10. box
11. sinner
12. Me
13. eat
15. Pharisee
17. hairs
18. Go
20. ointment
21. washed
22. anoint
23. owed

Down
1. came
2. water
3. say

4. pence
5. invitation
7. weeping
9. love
10. both
12. Master
14. kissed
16. Simon
19. oil

C. (Possible titles)
The Parable of the Sower
The Sower and the Seed
Seeds and Soil
Hearts that Bring Forth Fruit
Four Kinds of Ground

D. (Answers interchangeable within Roman numeral sections)

I. A. The fowls of the air eat the good seed
B. It is trodden down.
C. It is like people who hear, but will not believe and be saved.

II. A. As soon as the seed springs up, it withers away.
B. It lacks moisture.
C. It is like people who believe, but in the time of temptation fall away.

III. A. The good seed is choked.
B. They bring no fruit to perfection.
C. It is like people who are choked with the cares, riches, and pleasures of this life.

IV. A. The good seed brings forth fruit.
B. It is like people who hear the Word and obey it.
C. It is like people who have an honest and good heart.

LESSON 12
Jesus Calms and Heals

I. Preparing to Read

Pointer Questions

1. Whom and what did Jesus calm?
2. Whom did Jesus heal?

II. Reader

"How could the man possessed with devils live where people were buried? [The dead bodies were placed in caves or openings that could be entered.]

"To what pit did the devils beg Jesus not to send them? [The bottomless pit that is the home of Satan and his demons. They knew Jesus has power to send them there. In the final judgment they will be cast into the lake of fire forever and never be able to come out.]

"Of what do you think the people were afraid when they asked Jesus to leave? [Perhaps it was a fear of the unknown, stirred by this power that they could not understand. Perhaps they were afraid they would lose more pigs or other belongings by strange happenings.]

"What healed the woman who touched the hem of Jesus' garment? [her faith in Jesus' power]"

III. Workbook

Review the apostles' names.

ANSWER KEY

A.
1. b
2. c
3. a
4. b
5. d
6. b
7. a
8. b
9. a
10. d
11. b
12. d
13. a
14. d
15. c
16. d
17. c
18. b

B. (Individual work)

C.
1. a woman who had a disease twelve years
2. many people
3. the man healed of many devils
4. Jesus
5. all the people
6. the people
7. a storm of wind
8. the disciples
9. Jesus
10. the man with many devils

D.
1. B
2. A
3. A
4. B
5. A
6. A
7. B
8. B
9. B
10. B
11. A
12. A

E.
1. X
2.
3. X
4.
5.

LESSON 13
Jesus Shows His Power and Glory

I. Preparing to Read

Pointer Questions

1. How did Jesus show His power?
2. How did Jesus show His glory?

II. Reader

"How do you think the disciples lived when they went without food, extra clothes, or money? [They trusted God to provide for them, and God moved people to share with them along the way.]

"Why was Herod troubled to think John the Baptist had risen from the dead? [Herod was the one who had John killed. Perhaps to think that John could rise from the dead made Herod feel guilty for killing someone so great.]"

III. Workbook

Discuss question 4 in part A with the class. Help the children to recognize the things an ordinary person could not do as proof of Christ's deity.

ANSWER KEY

A. 1. a. John the Baptist
 b. Elijah
 c. one of the old prophets
2. the Christ of God
3. My beloved Son
4. a. He gave them power to cast out all devils and to cure diseases.
 b. He healed the ones who needed healing.
 c. All the people ate and were filled, yet there was food left.
 d. As He prayed, the look on His face changed and His clothes were white and shining.
 e. A voice out of the cloud said, "This is My beloved Son; hear Him."

B.

1. a	5. a
2. b	6. a
3. c	7. c
4. c	8. c

C. (Possible answers)
1. A widow who was willing to use the last of her meal and oil to feed Elijah found that there was always more as long as the famine lasted.
2. A woman who was in debt borrowed many vessels and poured her one pot of oil into them. There was enough oil to fill all the vessels.
3. A man brought some food to Elisha. Elisha's servant thought it would not reach for one hundred men; but they all had enough, and there was some left.

D.

1. 3	8. 2	15. 3
2. 4	9. 1	16. 2
3. 4	10. 4	17. 2
4. 4	11. 3	18. 2
5. 3	12. 2	19. 2
6. 3	13. 2	20. 4
7. 2	14. 3	21. 1

LESSON 14
Jesus Teaches the Disciples

I. Preparing to Read

Pointer Questions

1. Why did James and John suggest calling fire down from heaven?
2. What were the disciples to do if the people did not receive them in a city where they went to preach?

II. Reader

"What does *delivered* mean? What did Jesus mean when He said the Son of Man would be delivered into the hands of men? [When one is delivered *from* something, he is set free from it. When one is delivered *to* somebody, he is given or turned over to him. Jesus would be turned over to men for them to do to Him what they wanted.]

"When did Elijah command fire to come down from heaven to kill someone? [2 Kings 1:1–15]

"How can the dead bury the dead? [Someone who is interested only in the things of this life is spiritually dead. Jesus wanted the man to whom He said this, to follow Jesus as the most important thing and let the earthly things to those who did not have spiritual interests.]"

III. Workbook

Review the apostles' names.

ANSWER KEY

A. 1. a. one man
b. pleading
2. a. Jesus
b. kindly
3. a. John
b. disapproving
4. a. Jesus
b. rebuking
5. a. James and John
b. questioning
6. a. a man
b. eagerly
7. a. the seventy men
b. excited
8. a. Jesus
b. thankful

B. 1. ~~daughter~~, son
2. ~~afraid~~, grieved
3. ~~prisons~~, hands
4. ~~richest~~, greatest
5. ~~condemned~~, great
6. ~~Peter~~, John
7. ~~fifty~~, seventy
8. ~~fire~~, scorpions

C. (Individual work)

D. 1. c
2. c
3. a
4. c
5. a
6. c
7. b
8. c
9. a

Gradebook: 38 points, counting one point for each number in part B and excluding part E

LESSON 15
Lessons on Love and Prayer

I. Preparing to Read

Pointer Questions

1. What did the Law say about love?
2. What story did Jesus tell to teach a lesson about prayer?

II. Reader

"What did the story of the good Samaritan teach about love? [A neighbor is anyone with whom we have a contact, so we should love everyone.]

What did the story of the man asking for bread at midnight teach about prayer? [We should not stop praying if God does not seem to answer right away.]

"What did the story of fathers giving gifts to their sons teach about prayer? [God loves to give gifts and wants us to ask for what we need.]"

III. Workbook

ANSWER KEY

A.
1. He asked the question *to tempt Jesus.*
2. Jesus *asked him a question.*
3. The man was on his way to *Jericho.*
4. *A priest and a Levite* passed that way.
5. *A Samaritan* stopped and helped him.
6. He *bandaged the wounds,* pouring in oil and wine.
7. He *took care of the man* at the inn.
8. He *gave money for the care* of the man when he left.
9. *Martha* received Jesus into her house.
10. She *prepared the meal.*
11. Mary *sat at Jesus' feet* to listen to Him.
12. He would get up and give him bread because *he kept asking* for it.

B.

1.	no	6.	no
2.	no	7.	yes
3.	yes	8.	no
4.	no	9.	yes
5.	no	10.	yes

C.

1.	c	11.	c
2.	b	12.	e
3.	a	13.	b
4.	e	14.	a
5.	d	15.	d
6.	b	16.	e
7.	d	17.	a
8.	e	18.	b
9.	c	19.	c
10.	a	20.	d

LESSON 16
Jesus Talks to the Hypocrites

I. Preparing to Read

Pointer Questions

1. In what way were the Pharisees hypocrites?
2. Why did the scribes and Pharisees want Jesus to say many things?

II. Reader

Test the children's comprehension and memory with this oral quiz. Have them write the word or phrase for each blank as you read the sentences.

1. People said Jesus cast out devils by the chief of ____. (devils)
2. Only the power of ____ can cast out devils. (God)

3. A woman blessed the ____ of Jesus for having such a wonderful Son. (mother)
4. Jesus said those who hear the ____ and keep it are more blessed. (Word of God)
5. Jesus said that evil generation was looking for a ____. (sign)
6. The Queen of Sheba came from the farthest part of the earth to hear the wisdom of ____. (Solomon)
7. The men of Nineveh repented at the preaching of ____. (Jonah)
8. The Pharisee noticed that Jesus did not ____ before he ate. (wash)
9. Jesus said the Pharisees' ____ parts were full of greediness and wickedness. (inward)
10. Jesus said the Pharisees were like ____ that could not be seen which men walk over. (graves)
11. Jesus said, "Woe to you ____! for you load men with heavy burdens." (lawyers)
12. The lawyers took away the ____ of knowledge. (key)

III. Workbook

Review the apostles' names.

ANSWER KEY

A.
1. f
2. h
3. g
4. e
5. i
6. c
7. b
8. a
9. d
10. n
11. o
12. p
13. k
14. m
15. j
16. l

B.
1. 4 (walks through dry places, seeking rest)
2. 11 (He did not wash before eating.)
3. 7 (rise up and condemn that generation)
4. 17 (so He would say something for which they could accuse Him)
5. 9 (They were not willing to repent.)
6. 14 (graves)
7. 2 (If he did that, he would be working against himself.)
8. 6 (an evil generation)
9. 16 (the key of knowledge)
10. 5 (those who hear the word of God and keep it)
11. 15 (one of the lawyers)
12. 2 (God)
13. 12 (They made the outside clean and left the inside unclean.)
14. 6 (the sign of Jonah the prophet)
15. 7 (Jesus)

C.
1. c
2. b
3. c

D. (Words to be crossed out)
1. cover
2. here
3. worse
4. great
5. does
6. give
7. touch
8. key
9. bead
10. bear

LESSON 17
Jesus Teaches His Disciples

I. Preparing to Read

Pointer Questions

1. Whom did God call a fool?
2. What examples did Jesus use to teach the people that God would provide their food and clothes?

II. Reader

"Who can kill the body but do no more? Who is able to kill and then cast into hell?

"What things did Jesus tell the disciples not to think about? [their words before rulers, their food and clothes] Should people really not think about the things they are going to say or about their food and clothes? [Jesus was teaching His disciples not to have these earthly things uppermost in their minds and worry about them.]"

III. Workbook

ANSWER KEY

A.
1. ~~soon~~, seen
2. ~~now~~, not
3. ~~hear~~, fear
4. ~~forbidden~~, forgotten
5. ~~hours~~, hairs
6. ~~answer~~, teach
7. ~~barns~~, things
8. ~~suit~~, soul
9. ~~worry~~, wear
10. ~~show~~, grow
11. ~~wickedly~~, wonderfully
12. ~~hand~~, have
13. ~~frock~~, flock
14. ~~hate~~, have
15. ~~wanting~~, watching
16. ~~pray~~, repent

B. (Individual work)

C. (Individual response; probably *X* for each number)

D. (Typical answers)
1. 10
2. yes
3. no
4. feet, legs, heart, health, love, the Scriptures
5. thank Him

LESSON 18
Jesus Heals, Warns, and Teaches

I. Preparing to Read

Pointer Questions

1. Why did the ruler of the synagogue not like it that Jesus healed the woman?
2. Whom did Jesus say should be invited when one makes a feast?

II. Reader

"What did Jesus mean by the narrow gate? [The way to heaven requires one to give up his selfish interests, and so it is compared to a narrow gate that is not easy to go through. The many who seek to enter in and cannot are those who are not willing to obey the Lord but insist on their own way through life.]

"Why did Jesus call Herod a fox? [A fox is a sneaky animal, and Herod was known as a sly, tricky character.]"

III. Workbook

ANSWER KEY

A.
1. b
2. c
3. a
4. a
5. c
6. b
7. a
8. b
9. c
10. b
11. c
12. a
13. c
14. c
15. a

B.
1. The woman *glorified God* when she was healed.
2. He said, "*There are six days in which to work.* Come to be healed then."
3. They *took their animals to give them water.*
4. They were *ashamed.*
5. People will come from the *east, west, north, and south.*
6. He would have *gathered her children together* as a hen gathers her brood.
7. *They would not let Him.*
8. They would *kill Him.*

C.
1. as a hen doth gather her brood
2. like a serpent, like worms of the earth
3. like as corn is sifted in a sieve
4. like a wave of the sea
5. like a river day and night
6. like a ball into a large country
7. like a dove
8. like the troubled sea

D. infirmity
immediately
synagogue
angry
hypocrite

Gradebook: 45 points, counting two for each sentence answer in part B

LESSON 19
Forgiveness and Salvation Bring Joy

I. Preparing to Read

Pointer Questions

1. What excuses were given for not going to the supper?
2. What happened to the younger son's money?

II. Reader

"What did the great supper in Jesus' story stand for? [heaven]

"Do you think the father heard the son's statement that he was not worthy to be called his son? [He may have heard, but that did not bother him. He loved his son so much that it did not matter what the son had done in the past. If he now realized how foolish he had been and was sorry, the father wanted him back as a son.]

"Did the older son love his brother?"

III. Workbook

ANSWER KEY

A.
1. b
2. c
3. a
4. a
5. c
6. d
7. b
8. d
9. b
10. d
11. c
12. a
13. d
14. a
15. d
16. b
17. d
18. c

B.
1. The Great Supper
2. The Lost Sheep
3. The Lost Coin
4. The Lost Son

C. (A drawing illustrating one of the four stories named above)

D.
1. bread
2. suit
3. excused
4. oxen
5. lanes
6. hedges
7. interested
8. forsake
9. candle
10. neighbors
11. worthy
12. kissed

LESSON 20
The Rich Man and Lazarus

I. Preparing to Read

Pointer Questions

1. Why did the Pharisees make fun of the things Jesus said?
2. What could the rich man see from hell?

II. Reader

"Why did the steward mark down the amounts the debtors owed his master? [so they would pay more readily] Why did the master praise the steward for this? [because payment was made that may not otherwise have been received]

"How would Moses and the prophets tell the rich man's brothers not to go to hell? [The things Moses and the prophets said were written in the Scriptures. If the men heeded what the Bible says, they would not go to hell.]"

III. Workbook

ANSWER KEY

A.
1. true
2. false
3. true
4. false
5. false
6. false
7. true
8. false
9. true
10. false
11. true
12. false
13. false
14. false
15. true
16. true

B.
1. Satan's
2. no
3. Satan's
4. God's

C.
1. a
2. c
3. a
4. b
5. b
6. a
7. b
8. b
9. c
10. a
11. c
12. c
13. a
14. a
15. c
16. b
17. c
18. a
19. c
20. b

D. "For I reckon that the sufferings of this present time are not worthy to be compared with the glory which shall be revealed in us" (Romans 8:18)

LESSON 21
Jesus Teaches Great Lessons

I. Preparing to Read

Pointer Questions

1. When were the ten lepers healed?
2. Jesus compared the time of His coming to what other times?

II. Reader

"What did Jesus say could be done if one has faith as a grain of mustard seed? [A tree would obey the command to be plucked up and planted in the sea.] Do you know of anybody who has done that? [Faith does not ask God to do something just to see if He will do it. That is tempting God. A person who has true faith understands what is right to ask for, and when he asks, he really believes God will give what he needs. God does great things for such people.]

"What healed the lepers? [Their faith. If they had had no faith, they would have thought Jesus must heal them before they start off to show themselves to the priests.]"

III. Workbook

ANSWER KEY

A.
1. It would be worse to *cause a little one to sin.*
2. a. They should be careful *to do all that Jesus*

commands. (or) They should be careful *not to offend others.*

b. They should be careful *not to let others offend them.*

3. *They felt a need* for more faith. (or) They knew *it would not be easy to keep on being kind* to someone who is mean.
4. Even with a *small faith* a person can believe and obey Jesus. (or) *One needs faith as a grain of mustard seed.*
5. They asked Jesus to *have mercy on them.*
6. He told them to go *show themselves to the priests.*
7. One man turned back *to thank Jesus.*
8. He compared His coming to *lightning.*
9. a. He compared it to *the time of Noah.*
   b. He compared it to *the days of Lot.*

B. 1. offend
2. cannot, another, millstone, into
3. plucked, planted
4. sycamine
5. unprofitable
6. loud, voice, down
7. Samaritans, Jews
8. Son of Man
9. Sodom
10. eagles

C. (Individual work)

Gradebook: 44 points, counting two for each sentence answer in part A

LESSON 22
Whom Can Jesus Help?

I. Preparing to Read

Pointer Questions

1. Why did the unjust judge help the widow?
2. How could the rich ruler have gained treasure in heaven?

II. Reader

"How does a little child receive something? [Little children usually accept things as others tell them. They do not think they are better or wiser than others. Grown people likewise must accept what the Bible says without arguing or changing it to suit themselves.]

"Is it possible for a rich man to enter the kingdom of heaven? [It is easier for a camel to go through a needle's eye, which is impossible with man. With God it is possible.]

"Why did the blind man call Jesus 'Son of David'? [Joseph and Mary were of the family line of David; so Jesus too was a descendant of David.]"

III. Workbook

Review the apostles' names.

ANSWER KEY

A.
1. city, care, certain, city, came, continual, call
2. Pharisee, publican, pray, people, possess, proud, put
3. touch, them, tell
4. easier, eye, enter, ends
5. twelve, to, that, true, treated, third, telling
6. road, rebuked, receive, received

B.
1. Pharisee
2. Pharisee
3. Publican
4. Publican
5. Pharisee
6. Pharisee
7. Pharisee
8. Pharisee
9. Publican
10. Pharisee
11. Publican
12. Publican
13. Publican
14. Pharisee
15. Publican
16. Pharisee
17. Publican
18. Pharisee

C.
1. b
2. b
3. a
4. a
5. b
6. a
7. a
8. c

LESSON 23
Zacchaeus and the Nobleman

I. Preparing to Read

Pointer Questions

1. In what way was Zacchaeus the son of Abraham?
2. What is a pound?

II. Reader

Have the children write *true* or *false* for the sentences in this oral quiz.

1. Zacchaeus lived at Jericho. (T)
2. Zacchaeus was a Pharisee. (F)
3. Zacchaeus was very rich. (T)
4. Zacchaeus lived in a tree house. (F)
5. Zacchaeus asked Jesus to come to his home. (F)
6. Zacchaeus was afraid to take Jesus to his house. (F)
7. Zacchaeus was a sinner. (T)
8. Zacchaeus was sorry for his sins. (T)
9. Zacchaeus gave all of his things to the poor. (F)
10. If Zacchaeus took anything wrongfully, he gave back four times as much as he took. (T)

11. A nobleman went to a far country to receive a kingdom. (T)
12. The nobleman took his ten servants along. (F)
13. He gave each servant a talent of money. (F)
14. All the servants pleased their master by the way they used the money. (F)
15. Jesus went away to receive a kingdom for Himself. (T)

Discussion

"Where has Jesus gone to receive His kingdom? [heaven] What gifts has He given men to use for Him? [Abilities to preach and teach to bring others to the kingdom. Also, gifts of life, health and strength, and material provisions that we may carry on all the ordinary activities of life to glorify Him.]"

III. Workbook

The reader does not give the answer to question 7 in part A. Include it in class discussion if you think the children will need help with it.

Also, discuss the subject of part C.

ANSWER KEY

A. 1. a. Zacchaeus was *short.*
b. *Many people crowded* around Jesus.
2. He ran ahead and *climbed a tree.*
3. Jesus talked to him and *came to his house.*
4. They complained because *Zachaeus was a sinner.*
5. Everyone who is *faithful to the Lord* is a child of Abraham.
6. The nobleman went to *a far country.*
7. Jesus went to *heaven.*

B.
1.
2.
3. X
4. X
5.
6.
7. X
8. X
9.
10.
11. X
12. X
13. X
14. X
15. X

C. (Possible answers)
Jesus has given food. People can share it to show God's love.
Jesus has given health and physical strength. People can use it in activities that help others.
Jesus has given the Bible. People can share the message so others will be saved.
Jesus has given the Holy Spirit. People can let the Spirit direct their lives to bring glory to God.
Jesus has given understanding and ability to communicate. People can witness to others about God.

D. (Individual work)

LESSON 24
Jesus at Jerusalem

I. Preparing to Read

Pointer Questions

1. What did the people do to show their respect and love to Jesus?
2. What made Jesus weep?

II. Reader

"How do you think it would be to ride a colt on which no one had ever sat? [It would probably be hard to stay on because the animal would not be used to carrying people.] Why do you think there was no problem this time? [God controlled the situation. Maybe the animal sensed the presence and will of its Creator.]

"Why could the Jewish leaders not answer Jesus' question? [One answer would get them in trouble with the people, and the other would trap them into admitting Jesus' deity.]"

III. Workbook

ANSWER KEY

A.

3	6	15	18
5	7	11	17
2	8	14	19
4	9	12	16
1	10	13	20

B.
1. They praised God because of the *mighty works* they had seen.
2. Jesus wept because *the people would not come to Him* for mercy and *would have to receive great punishment.*
3. They did not know how to get rid of Jesus because the *people were eager to hear Him.*
4. Any answer they could give would *trap* them.
5. He told the story to *help the Jews realize* that they were going to kill God's Son.

C.
1. f
2. e
3. c
4. g
5. d
6. a
7. h
8. b

D.
1. disciples
2. colt
3. multitude
4. immediately
5. surround
6. thieves
7. authority
8. persuaded
9. parable
10. vineyard

LESSON 25
Jesus Answers Jewish Leaders

I. Preparing to Read

Pointer Questions

1. In what belief did the scribes and Sadducees differ?
2. Who threw the most money into the treasury?

II. Reader

"What catch might there have been in the question about tax? What if Jesus had said they should not pay? [That would have gotten Him into trouble with the Roman law, and maybe the Romans would have killed Him.] What if Jesus would have told them outright to pay tax? [The Jews disliked paying taxes enough that many of them might have turned against Jesus.]"

III. Workbook

ANSWER KEY

A. 1. b
2. c
3. a

B. watch and pray

C. (Any eight)
There will be wars and commotions.
Nations shall rise against nation.
Kingdom shall rise against kingdom.
There will be earthquakes.
There will be famines.
There will be diseases.
There will be fearful sights and great signs from heaven.
Christ's followers will be persecuted.
They will be put into prisons.
They will be brought before kings and rulers for Jesus' sake.

D.

1.
2. X
3. X
4.
5. X
6. X
7. X
8.
9.
10. X
11. X
12. X
13. X
14.
15.
16. X
17.
18. X
19. X
20. X

LESSON 26
The Passover

I. Preparing to Read

Pointer Questions

1. Which disciple did Satan enter into?
2. Which disciple did Satan desire to have?

II. Reader

"Jesus would deliver His people from sin. Judas promised to deliver Jesus to the chief priests. What does *deliver* mean in each sentence? ["to free from bondage"; "to hand over to another"]

"Why did Judas intend to betray Jesus when the multitude was absent? [So many people loved Jesus that it could have caused a great uproar if they tried to take Jesus when everybody was around.]

"When would the Passover be fulfilled in the kingdom of God? [One purpose of the Passover was a looking forward to the sacrifice of Jesus' blood. When Jesus died, the Passover was fulfilled.]"

III. Workbook

See that songbooks are available for reference in doing part E. You may want to use this opportunity to acquaint the children with the use of a topical index.

ANSWER KEY

A.
1. b
2. c
3. a, d
4. c
5. a
6. a
7. b
8. c
9. b
10. a

B.
1. a. It helped them remember their *deliverance from Egypt.*
   b. It helped them look forward to the sacrifice of *Jesus' blood.*
2. *Satan entered into his heart.*
3. Judas loved *money* more than he loved Jesus.
4. The great men were to be *as the younger* and as *servants.*
5. Peter said he was ready to *go to prison and to death* for Jesus.

C.
1. c
2. a
3. d
4. e
5. g
6. b
7. f

D. This do in remembrance of Me.

E. (Answers may vary greatly.)

LESSON 27
Jesus in Gethsemane

I. Preparing to Read

Pointer Questions

1. Who was first to say that Peter had been with Jesus?
2. What reminded Peter that Jesus had said he would deny Him?

II. Reader

"What did Jesus mean when He said, 'Remove this cup from Me'? [He knew the difficult experience that was coming to Him, and He compared it to a bitter cup to drink. He wanted to have it taken away if God would be willing to do so.]

"Why did the elders, chief priests, and scribes say, 'What need have we of more witnesses?' [Jesus had said clearly enough that He is the Son of God. They thought that was reason enough to have Him killed, for it is very serious for a man to claim to be God.]"

III. Workbook

Can the children still name the twelve apostles?

ANSWER KEY

A.
1. Mount, Olives
2. disciples
3. Pray
4. a person can throw a stone
5. kneeled down
6. willing
7. Yours
8. angel, strength
9. earnestly
10. sweat
11. sleeping
12. pray
13. Judas
14. kiss
15. ear, servant
16. Three
17. rooster crowed
18. turned, looked
19. remembered
20. had declared he would not do
21. sorry
22. bitterly
23. hit
24. blindfolded
25. Christ

B.
1. A *fire* was started in the middle of the hall.
2. He was in an *agony*, and His sweat was like drops of blood.
3. God sent an *angel* to strengthen Him.
4. They asked if they should kill with the *sword*. (or) Peter took his *sword* and cut off a man's ear.
5. Jesus *told* Peter to put the sword back, and He *healed the ear.*

C.
1. inquire
2. persecute
3. absent
4. devour
5. audience
6. council
7. agony
8. betray
9. converted
10. deny

Gradebook: 50 points, counting two for each sentence answer in part B

LESSON 28
Jesus Is Tried and Crucified

I. Preparing to Read

Pointer Questions

1. Why was Herod glad to see Jesus?
2. What did Jesus say when He was crucified?

II. Reader

"What had Jesus said about the tax question? [He said, "Give to Caesar the things that are Caesar's, and to God the things that are God's."

"Why was Jesus taken to Pilate? [Pilate was the Roman governor and had the authority to say when a person should be killed.] Why was Jesus sent to Herod? [Jesus was from Galilee, and Herod ruled Galilee. Pilate did not see any reason to kill Jesus and was glad to let somebody else be responsible for the case.]

"Why do you think Jesus would not answer Herod? [Herod was not interested in following Jesus, but was asking out of curiosity about the miracles Jesus could do.]"

III. Workbook

ANSWER KEY

A.
1. Pilate
2. Galilee
3. governor
4. yes
5. yes
6. some miracle
7. no
8. chief priests and scribes
9. no
10. before
11. no
12. Barabbas
13. at the Passover
14. a murderer
15. Calvary
16. two
17. thieves
18. vinegar
19. three
20. above Jesus' head

B.
1. Jesus turned to them and said, "Daughters of Jerusalem, do not weep for Me. Weep for yourselves and for your children."
2. He prayed for them, saying, "Father, forgive them, for they do not know what they do." (or) Jesus had no hard feelings toward those who crucified Him.
3. Herod asked Jesus many things, but Jesus would not answer him.

C.
1. Jesus had said, "Give to Caesar the things that are Caesar's, and to God the things that are God's."
2. Jesus had done no evil, and Barabbas was a murderer.

D.
1. c
2. b
3. b
4. c
5. c
6. b
7. a
8. a
9. b
10. a

E.
1. governor
2. fiercer
3. Galilean
4. cruelly
5. murderer
6. immediately

LESSON 29
Jesus' Death, Burial, and Resurrection

I. Preparing to Read

Pointer Questions

1. What did each of the two thieves on the crosses ask of Jesus?
2. Who buried Jesus?

II. Reader

"How do you know the one thief believed that Jesus was a king? [He said, "Remember me when You come into Your kingdom."]

"Did all the men of the Jewish council want Jesus crucified? [No, Joseph believed in Jesus.]"

III. Workbook

ANSWER KEY

A.
1. He promised the thief that *he would be with Him in paradise that day.*
2. The sun was darkened *three* hours.
3. They *followed Joseph and saw* where he buried Jesus.
4. *Two men in shining clothes* told them Jesus was risen. (or) *Angels* told them Jesus was risen.

B.

Across

1. council
4. paradise
7. insistent
9. condemnation
12. mustard
14. betray
15. wondrous
16. deny
17. brimstone

Down

2. converted
3. lo
5. absent
6. centurion
8. agony
10. audience
11. stern
13. devour
14. bosom

C.
1. us
2. die
3. paradise
4. three, veil
5. cried, hands
6. centurion, righteous
7. believed

8. Pilate
9. lay
10. week, spices
11. men, clothes
12. dead, risen

D. (Any order)

Simon	Matthew
Andrew	Thomas
James	James
John	Simon
Philip	Judas
Bartholomew	Judas

LESSON 30
The Ascension

I. Preparing to Read

Pointer Questions

1. Why were the disciples afraid when Jesus appeared among them?
2. How did Jesus prove to them that He was not just a spirit?

II. Reader

"Why were the two disciples puzzled about the things that had just happened? [They had been sure Jesus was to redeem Israel, but instead He had been killed and buried. Also puzzling was the report that His body was no longer in the grave.]

"Were the disciples going to Emmaus two of the apostles? [No, because when they recognized Jesus, they hurried back to Jerusalem, where they found the eleven apostles. Judas was absent.]"

III. Workbook

ANSWER KEY

A. (Important points)
Jesus' walk with the disciples going to Emmaus
Their recognition of Jesus and return to Jerusalem
Jesus' appearance to the disciples
Jesus' assurance by showing His hands and feet, and by eating
The ascension

B.
1. c
2. a
3. b
4. c
5. c

C.
1. d
2. h
3. i
4. j
5. b
6. l
7. o
8. n
9. k
10. c
11. a
12. f
13. p
14. g
15. m
16. k
17. e
18. q

TEST

ANSWER KEY

A.
1. c
2. a
3. e
4. g
5. b
6. f
7. d
8. h
9. i
10. n
11. j
12. l
13. m
14. o
15. k

B.
1. F
2. F
3. T
4. F
5. F
6. T
7. T
8. F
9. T
10. F
11. F
12. T

C.
1. compel
2. agony
3. indebted
4. Beelzebub
5. wondrous
6. millstone
7. absent
8. paradise
9. justified
10. devour

D. (One Judas circled)

Simon
Andrew
James
John
Philip
Bartholomew
Matthew
Thomas
James
Simon
Judas
Judas

Gradebook: 50 test points